MEASURING AND FUNDING CORPORATE LIABILITIES FOR RETIREE HEALTH BENEFITS

AN EBRI-ERF POLICY STUDY

This study was prepared in cooperation with the Employee Benefit Research Institute-Education and Research Fund by the staff of Milliman & Robertson, Inc., in memoriam to Wendell A. Milliman, a founder of the firm. Authors of the study are Phyllis A. Doran, F.S.A., Kenneth D. MacBain, F.S.A., and William A. Reimert, F.S.A., consulting actuaries with Milliman & Robertson, Inc.

EBRI

EBRI-ERF
EMPLOYEE BENEFIT RESEARCH INSTITUTE
EDUCATION AND RESEARCH FUND

© 1987 Employee Benefit Research Institute
2121 K Street, NW, Suite 600
Washington, DC 20037-2121
(202) 659-0670

All rights reserved. No part of this publication may be used or reproduced in any manner whatsoever without permission in writing from the Employee Benefit Research Institute except in the case of brief quotations embodied in news articles, critical articles, or reviews. The ideas and opinions expressed in this publication are those of the authors and do not necessarily represent the views of the Employee Benefit Research Institute, the EBRI Education and Research Fund, or its trustees, members, or associates.

Library of Congress Cataloging in Publication Data

Main entry under title:

Measuring and funding corporate liabilities for retiree
   health benefits.

   1. Insurance, Health—United States—Accounting.
   2. Postemployment benefits—United States—Accounting.
   3. Liabilities (Accounting).   I. Employee Benefit Research Institute (Washington, D.C.).   Education and Research Fund.
   HG9396.M4   1987   657'.75   87-24534
   ISBN 0-86643-054-7 (pbk.)

Printed in the United States of America

Table of Contents

	Page
List of Tables	vii
List of Charts	xiii
Foreword	xv
Preface	xix
Growth in Medical Care Spending	xix
Financial Accounting Standards Board	xx
Acquisitions and Shutdowns	xx
Costs Relating to Early Retirement and Corporate Restructuring	xxi
Funding	xxi
Dedication	xxv
About the Authors	xxvi
Executive Summary	xxvii
Background	xxvii
Current Status; Advance Funding Considerations	
Summary and Major Findings	xxx
Size of Liabilities; Medical Cost Trends; Sensitivity to Other Factors; Medicare Changes; Prefunding Techniques and Costs; Benefit Security	
Study Objectives and Methodology	xxxvi
Description of Model Groups; Study Methodology	
Issues Not Covered in This Study	xxxviii

PART ONE
PRESENT VALUES OF FUTURE BENEFITS (CLOSED GROUP)

Chapter I
Present Value of Future Benefits—Basic Results	3
Development of Present Values of Future Benefits	3

Projection of Covered Population by Year; Per Capita Plan Costs; Total Plan Costs by Year; Present Value of Future Benefits
Present Value of Future Benefits for Model Groups 4
Discussion of Economic Assumptions 6
Trend; Discount Rate; Relationship of Trend and Discount Rate to GNP Growth

Chapter II
Sensitivity of Benefit Values to Changes in Assumptions 11
   Economic Assumptions 11
   Early Retirement Rates 11
   Mortality 13
   Eligibility for Early Retirement 13
   Reductions in Coverage Prior to Age 65 15
   Other Coverage for Spouses 15

Chapter III
Effects of Plan Design and Benefit Changes 17
   Benefit Plan 17
   Future Changes in Benefits 18
     Freeze in Retiree Contributions; Changes in Medicare

Chapter IV
Accrual and Vesting of Benefits 23
   Alternative Accrual Methods 24
     Accrual at Retirement; Accrual at Eligibility for Retirement; Ratable Accrual from Date of Hire to Age 65; Ratable Accrual from Date of Hire to Earliest Eligibility for Retirement; Ratable Accrual over Fixed Period of Service
   Cessation of Employer Operations 25

PART TWO
FUNDING SCENARIOS (OPEN GROUP)

Chapter V
Methods for Funding and Expensing of Retiree Medical Benefits 33
   Retiree Medical Funding Methods (Pension Techniques) 33
     Entry Age Normal; Projected Unit Credit; Aggregate

Pattern of Normal Costs	34
Funding of Initial Liability	35
Modified Advance Funding Methods for Retiree Medical Benefits	36
Unprojected Unit Credit; Unit Credit with No Trend or Discount Rate; Projected Unit Credit with Trend Equal to Per Capita GNP Growth Rate	
Expensing for Retiree Medical Benefits	37

Chapter VI
Funding Scenarios: General Approach	39
Open Group Assumptions	39
Economic Scenarios	41
Taxes	42

Chapter VII
Comparison of Funding Patterns	43
Annual Contributions	43
Comparison with Pay-As-You-Go Funding	44
Fund Accumulation	46
Costs Per Employee	

Chapter VIII
Comparison of Funding Adequacy	59
Benefit Liabilities	59
Funding Ratios	59
Full Funding Methods; Modified Advance Funding Methods	
Funding Ratios: Cessation of Employer Operations	62
Illustration of Funding Adequacy	63

PART THREE
PLAN DESIGN ISSUES

Chapter IX
Employer Plan Design Alternatives	71
Changes in Plan Design	71
Increases in Retiree Cost Sharing; Increases in Retiree Contributions; Utilization Management Programs; Multiple Options; Variation in Retiree Benefits by Length of Service	

Changes in the Nature of Benefit Commitments 74
    Defined Dollar Benefit; Defined Contribution

Chapter X
Changes in Employer Commitments: Funding and Vesting
Implications 77
    Benefit Adequacy 77
        Length of Service; Early Vesting; Early Retirement
        Subsidies; Dependent Coverage Subsidies
    Vesting and Portability 81
    Retiree Coverage Options 82
    Employee Funding Options 84

APPENDICES

Appendix A
Description of Major Assumptions 85

Appendix B
Funding Scenarios: Illustrative Annual Values 105
    Description 105

Appendix C
Funding Scenarios: Benefit Liabilities 163
    Description 163

Appendix D
Funding Scenarios: Illustrative Funding Ratios 171

List of Tables

Table   **Page**

Executive Summary

1	Present Value of Retiree Health Benefits, Sample Plan	xxxii
2	Allocation of Total Liability, Sample Plan	xxxii
3	Variation in Liabilities by Trend Scenario	xxxiii
4	Change in Employer Retiree Health Liabilities As Result of Changes in Key Variables, Based on Current Employees	xxxiv
5	Cost of Funding Retiree Medical Benefits	xxxv
6	Major Characteristics of Model Groups	xxxvii
7	Annual Projected Growth Rates	xxxviii

Chapter I
Present Value of Future Benefits (Closed Group)

I.1	Assumed Average First-Year Per Capita Plan Costs	4
I.2	Major Projection Assumptions	5
I.3	Present Value of Future Benefits and Current Payments	6
I.4	Allocation of Present Value of Future Benefits	7
I.5	Variation in Present Value of Future Benefits by Trend Scenario	10

Chapter II
Sensitivity of Benefit Values to Changes in Assumptions

II.1	Percent Change in Present Value of Future Benefits Due to Change in Average Trend	12
II.2	Effect of Doubling Early Retirement Rates on Present Value of Future Benefits for Current Employees	12
II.3	Effect of Reducing Mortality Rates on Present Value of Future Benefits for Current and Retired Employees	13
II.4	Effect of Five-Year Service Requirement on Present Value of Future Benefits for Current Employees	13

II.5	Effect of Reductions in Coverage Prior to Age 65 on Present Value of Future Benefits for Current Employees	14
II.6	Effect of Increase in Other Coverage for Spouses on Present Value of Future Benefits for Current and Retired Employees	14

Chapter III
Effects of Plan Design and Benefit Changes

III.1	Illustrative Costs by Type of Benefit Plan	17
III.2	Effect of Plan Changes on Present Value of Future Benefits	18
III.3	Effect of Freeze in Retiree Contributions on Employer-Paid Present Value of Future Benefits	19
III.4	Effect of Decline in Medicare Coverage Levels on Present Value of Future Benefits for Current Employees	20
III.5	Effect on Present Value of Future Benefits for Current Employees If Medicare Coverage Becomes Secondary	21

Chapter IV
Accrual and Vesting of Benefits

IV.1	Illustration of Alternative Accrual Methods	25
IV.2	Comparison of Accrued Benefit Liabilities under Alternative Accrual Methods	26
IV.3	Comparison of Accrued Benefit Liabilities for Current Employees: Continuation of Operations vs. Cessation	27
IV.4	Comparison of Accrued Benefit Liabilities for Current Employees: Continuation of Operations vs. Cessation; Early Retirement Rates = Twice Original Rates	28

Chapter VI
Funding Scenarios: General Approach

VI.1	Open Group Projection Results: Population Counts for Selected Years	40
VI.2	Summary of Economic Assumptions	42

Chapter VII
Comparison of Funding Patterns

VII.1	Comparison of Annual Contributions: Full Funding Methods, Group A (Stable), Medium Trend Scenario	44
VII.2	Comparison of Annual Contributions: Modified Advance Funding Methods, Group A (Stable), Medium Trend Scenario	45
VII.3	Comparison of Fund Accumulation: Full Funding Methods, Group A (Stable), Medium Trend Scenario	50
VII.4	Comparison of Fund Accumulation: Modified Advance Funding Methods, Group A (Stable), Medium Trend Scenario	52
VII.5	Initial Advance Funding Costs Per Employee, Medium Trend Scenario	52
VII.6	Comparison of Funding Costs Per Employee by Year, Projected Unit Credit—Minimum	
VII.6a	Group A (Stable—2% Growth)	53
VII.6b	Group F (Older—2% Decline)	53
VII.6c	Group F (Older—7% Decline)	54
VII.6d	Group H (New—2% Growth)	54

Chapter VIII
Comparison of Funding Adequacy

VIII.1	Accrued Ongoing Benefit Obligations, Group A (Stable), Medium Trend Scenario	60
VIII.2	Funding Ratios: Full Funding Methods, Group A (Stable), Medium Trend Scenario, Projected Unit Credit—Minimum	61
VIII.3	Funding Ratios: Modified Advance Funding Methods, Group A (Stable), Medium Trend Scenario, Unprojected Unit Credit—Minimum	62
VIII.4	Funding Ratios: Modified Advance Funding Methods, Group A (Stable), Medium Trend Scenario, Unit Credit with No Trend or Discount Rate—Minimum	63

VIII.5   Funding Ratios: Modified Advance Funding
         Methods, Group A (Stable), Medium Trend
         Scenario, Projected Unit Credit with Trend Equal
         to Per Capita GNP—Minimum   64

Chapter X
Changes in Employer Commitments:
Funding and Vesting Implications

X.1   Present Value of Future Medical Benefits for an
      Individual Retiring Today   78
X.2   Annual Level Dollar Contribution Required to Fully
      Fund Postretirement Medical Benefits   78
X.3   Illustrative Future Annual Per Capita Costs for
      Individual Retiring Today at Age 55   81

Appendix A
Description of Major Assumptions

A.1   Participant Data—Active Employees: Group A, Age
       and Years of Continuous Service   87
A.2   Participant Data—Active Employees: Group F, Age
       and Years of Continuous Service   88
A.3   Participant Data—Active Employees: Group H, Age
       and Years of Continuous Service   89
A.4   Participant Data—Inactive Participants: Group A ...   90
A.5   Participant Data—Inactive Participants: Group F ...   94
A.6   Participant Data—Inactive Participants: Group H ...   98
A.7   Percentage Increase in Salary for Continuing and
       New Employees 100
A.8   Percentage of Employees Married at Retirement 101
A.9   Sample Average Annual per Capita Costs by Age:
       First Year 101
A.10   Assumed Rates of Retirement 102
A.11   Sample Annual Separation Rates Per 100
       Employees: Group A 102
A.12   Sample Annual Rates Per 100 Employees: Group F   103
A.13   Sample Annual Rates Per 100 Employees: Group H   103

A.14	Assumed Age Distribution of New Entrants	104

Appendix B
Funding Scenarios: Illustrative Annual Values

B.1	Group A: Low Trend Scenario	107
B.2	Group A: Medium Trend Scenario	111
B.3	Group A: High Trend Scenario	117
B.4	Group F—2% Rate of Decline: Low Trend Scenario	121
B.5	Group F—2% Rate of Decline: Medium Trend Scenario	125
B.6	Group F—2% Rate of Decline: High Trend Scenario	131
B.7	Group F—7% Rate of Decline: Low Trend Scenario	135
B.8	Group F—7% Rate of Decline: Medium Trend Scenario	139
B.9	Group F—7% Rate of Decline: High Trend Scenario	145
B.10	Group H: Low Trend Scenario	149
B.11	Group H: Medium Trend Scenario	153
B.12	Group H: High Trend Scenario	159

Appendix C
Funding Scenarios: Benefit Liabilities

C.1	Group A: Low Trend Scenario	164
C.2	Group A: Medium Trend Scenario	164
C.3	Group A: High Trend Scenario	165
C.4	Group F—2% Rate of Decline: Low Trend Scenario	165
C.5	Group F—2% Rate of Decline: Medium Trend Scenario	166
C.6	Group F—2% Rate of Decline: High Trend Scenario	166
C.7	Group F—7% Rate of Decline: Low Trend Scenario	167
C.8	Group F—7% Rate of Decline: Medium Trend Scenario	167
C.9	Group F—7% Rate of Decline: High Trend Scenario	168
C.10	Group H: Low Trend Scenario	168
C.11	Group H: Medium Trend Scenario	169
C.12	Group H: High Trend Scenario	169

Appendix D
Funding Scenarios: Illustrative Funding Ratios

D.1	Group A: Low Trend Scenario	172
D.2	Group A: Medium Trend Scenario	176
D.3	Group A: High Trend Scenario	182
D.4	Group F—2% Rate of Decline: Low Trend Scenario	186
D.5	Group F—2% Rate of Decline: Medium Trend Scenario	190
D.6	Group F—2% Rate of Decline: High Trend Scenario	196
D.7	Group F—7% Rate of Decline: Low Trend Scenario	200
D.8	Group F—7% Rate of Decline: Medium Trend Scenario	204
D.9	Group F—7% Rate of Decline: High Trend Scenario	210
D.10	Group H: Low Trend Scenario	214
D.11	Group H: Medium Trend Scenario	218
D.12	Group H: High Trend Scenario	224

List of Charts

Chart		Page

Chapter VII
Comparison of Funding Patterns

VII.1	Comparison of Pay-As-You-Go and Full Funding Methods, Medium Trend Scenario	
VII.1a	Group A (Stable—2% Growth)	46
VII.1b	Group F (Older—2% Decline)	47
VII.1c	Group F (Older—7% Decline)	48
VII.1d	Group H (New—2% Growth)	49
VII.2	Range of Fund Accumulation for Full Funding Methods, Medium Trend Scenario	51
VII.3	Funding Costs As Percentage of Payroll by Year, Medium Trend Scenario	
VII.3a	Group A (Stable—2% Growth)	55
VII.3b	Group F (Older—2% Decline)	56
VII.3c	Group F (Older—7% Decline)	57
VII.3d	Group H (New—2% Growth)	58

Chapter VIII
Comparison of Funding Adequacy

Funding and Liabilities, Medium Trend Scenario: Continuation of Employer Operations and Cessation of Employer Operations

VIII.1	Group A (Stable—2% Growth)	
VIII.1a	Continuation	65
VIII.1b	Cessation	65
VIII.2	Group F (Older—2% Decline)	
VIII.2a	Continuation	66
VIII.2b	Cessation	66
VIII.3	Group F (Older—7% Decline)	
VIII.3a	Continuation	67
VIII.3b	Cessation	67
VIII.4	Group H (New—2% Growth)	
VIII.4a	Continuation	68
VIII.4b	Cessation	68

Foreword

Health insurance has always been one of the first employee benefits that employers provide as part of the employment package, reflecting the importance of health benefits to workers and to the unions that frequently represent them. Continuation of employer-provided health insurance into retirement has been a relatively common provision of medium and large employer plans during the past 20 years. In 1986, 76 percent of full-time health plan participants in medium and large establishments had coverage continued after early retirement; 90 percent of these had coverage continued after age 65.

As a matter of history, employment-based retiree health insurance has been treated as a year-to-year promise paid for as part of the same health care plan provided to active workers. Then, in response to changes in the economic environment and to a series of court decisions, the Financial Accounting Standards Board (FASB) began to focus on the provision of retiree health benefits as a longer-term promise and, therefore, as a liability.

Attention in recent years has increasingly focused on the nature of the promise and the extent of the liability as some employers have attempted to reduce the benefits they provide to retirees. The LTV Corporation's bankruptcy filing and the temporary end of retiree health benefits brought by that action drew Congress deeply into this issue and caused many parties to begin asking, "How big is this promise, and what are the implications of continuing to provide it as a pay-as-you-go benefit?"

In 1986 the U.S. Department of Labor released a study in which it estimated that benefits already promised to workers over age 40 would have a cost of $98 billion. Shortly thereafter, a report from the House Select Committee on Aging put the liability at closer to $2 trillion if all workers, and likely levels of health care inflation, were considered. FASB then made clear its intent to issue an accounting standard that would require that at least a portion of this liability be placed on the corporate balance sheet. EBRI senior researcher Deborah J. Chollet estimates that public and private employers providing retiree health benefits may be liable for an estimated $85 billion in unfunded commitments for current retirees alone.

"Booking"—or recognizing on the corporate balance sheet—even a part of the retiree liability could affect the value of corporations, their ability to borrow, and their willingness to provide retiree health benefits to future workers and retirees. The annual pay-as-you-go expense for some individual employers exceeds $800 million, with long-term liabilities for such employers running into the billions of dollars.

Some employers have said they may wish to put funds for retiree health benefits aside in advance as they do with pensions. Others may consider moving from the provision of an employer-paid health insurance plan to a defined contribution, cash accumulation account and limit the retiree health "promise" to making insurance available for purchase by retirees.

All employers that provide retiree health insurance should, at a minimum, determine the size of their company's liability for future benefits. While this may sound like an obvious point, a recent survey of large employers found that more than two-thirds have no idea how much these benefits might cost them after 1986 or how large their long-term liability is.

EBRI began working on the issue of retiree health insurance some years ago. When the Deficit Reduction Act of 1984 initially called for a study by the federal government, and the Tax Reform Act of 1986 extended the report's due date, EBRI made the decision to undertake research that might assist in that effort. The consulting actuarial firm of Milliman & Robertson, Inc., agreed to perform this pioneering study of the liability question, focusing on how employers might deal with the issue through funding, and how much alternative approaches might cost. This report presents the results of that work, which will be of great value to all parties concerned about keeping the promise of health insurance made to retirees.

All studies of this nature represent a certain degree of risk, since there are many ways to look at any issue. EBRI and Milliman & Robertson, Inc., invite comment and discussion on the study, consistent with the spirit in which it was produced: namely, to add a factual component to a debate over issues of great import and high emotion.

Milliman & Robertson, Inc., donated the staff work for this study to EBRI and its Education and Research Fund as a tribute to Wendell A. Milliman (1906–1976), a founder of the firm. On behalf of EBRI and all parties with an interest in this subject, I thank Milliman & Robertson, Inc., for their contribution and, in particular, actuaries Phyllis Doran, Kenneth MacBain, and William Reimert for the substantial effort and creativity they have invested in this important study.

DALLAS L. SALISBURY
President
Employee Benefit Research Institute

November 1987

Preface

The issues addressed in this study have major implications for the many employers that offer retiree health benefits, for policymakers concerned about the future of these programs, and for labor unions and organizations that represent the millions of active and retired workers that benefit from retiree health programs.

Growth in Medical Care Spending

As the authors show, if health care costs continue to increase at the rates they have in the recent past, relative to rates of growth in the Gross National Product (GNP), by the year 2035 health care spending would consume 100 percent of GNP! This is, of course, an impossible scenario; however, it illustrates the clear need to discover effective ways of controlling health care cost increases.

For companies that sponsor retiree health benefit plans, the costs of the programs now in place are likely to increase significantly. The authors estimate the growth in program costs using a range of reasonable assumptions about future increases in medical costs. These illustrations provide an indication of the rates of future increases in expenditures to be experienced by many corporations.

Most employers approach the adjustment for future inflation of pension and health benefits in significantly different ways, since the nature of the "promise" for these benefits is different. Few companies automatically index their pension benefits, out of concern for managing what might otherwise be open-ended liabilities. But retiree health programs promise medical benefits, for which costs have grown faster than any other category of consumer spending; employers are, in effect, promising fully indexed medical benefits. This study projects the impact of these future cost increases, providing a framework for assessing whether continuation at that level is a necessary and justifiable business decision. If corporations fail to take actions to modify the terms of their plans, the programs now in place will have a significant effect on future corporate profitability.

The study illustrates the effect on future liabilities that certain kinds of changes may produce. Changes in the level of benefit coverage can dramatically affect total liabilities; for example, a company with a $100 deductible and 80 percent reimbursement of medical costs may have a per capita retiree health expense that is two times that of a plan with a $500 deductible and 75 percent reimbursement. The study indicates the relative magnitude of per capita retiree health benefits for low, medium, and high levels of coverage.

The study also discusses efforts currently being taken by some employers to more tightly control future liabilities and attain a greater degree of predictability of future costs by modifying the nature of the benefit promise. An employer may attempt to limit the firm's financial obligation by promising a fixed dollar level of benefits, as opposed to the promise of reimbursing a portion of medical expenses. This fixed dollar approach raises a number of questions, such as: How, if at all, would the benefit be vested? What arrangements should be made for portability? What if the dollar benefit that is accumulated for a given worker includes allowances for spousal coverage, but the spouse dies before the covered worker retires? What about duplication of coverage where two working spouses are with firms that promise benefits in retirement? These issues and others are discussed, including the considerations in developing a benefit formula to deliver this type of benefit.

Financial Accounting Standards Board

The Financial Accounting Standards Board (FASB) is currently working on an "exposure draft" that could, for the first time, require employers to account for the liabilities for their retiree health promises to workers. Should FASB finalize such a rule, it will be necessary for all employers promising retiree health benefits to determine the value of these liabilities and incorporate some or all of these amounts into their corporate financial statements.

This study illustrates a range of liabilities for three hypothetical companies and indicates the annual expenditures required to expense or finance the related benefits during the terms of employment of the covered workers. These liabilities and annual financing costs, if reflected on companies' financial statements, would affect corporate earnings, corporate borrowing capacity, and the prices of corporate stocks and bonds.

Acquisitions and Shutdowns

These values may also affect multibillion-dollar decisions to acquire other companies or to cease operations. An important but frequently neglected consideration in valuing a company for potential acquisition is the value of liabilities for promised retiree health benefits. These are often significant but unrecognized liabilities; where attempts have been made to estimate their value, misunderstanding and confusion have often resulted. This study discusses the types of assumptions that can or should be made regarding future retiree health benefit costs, and how sensitive the estimated liabilities are to variations in assumptions.

When a company ceases operations or there is a plant shutdown, there may be some savings from benefits promised but not yet vested, and therefore not delivered, to current workers; but there can be an offsetting increase in liabilities due to the large number of employees that immediately become eligible for retirement benefits as a result of a plant shutdown.

Costs Relating to Early Retirement and Corporate Restructuring

An increasing number of America's corporations have been using special incentives for early retirement as a way of reducing their labor forces without resorting to layoffs. This study shows that for an individual retiring at age 55, the present value of the retiree health benefits promised by the company are two and one-half times the present value of those promised to an individual retiring at age 65. Thus, encouraging early retirement can double what are already large and rapidly growing expenses. Indeed, in some cases the present value of retiree health benefits promised to an early retiree can exceed the present value of the pension benefits promised to that same worker. Thus, the one-time offer of an early retirement window can cause the firm's retiree health benefit costs to skyrocket, a factor that has been largely unrecognized by many that have taken that route.

This study illustrates the costs of offering retiree health benefits where total employment is growing, declining, or stable. The illustration of what happens to a company with declining employment is particularly relevant to the many U.S. corporations that have been "downsizing," as well as to entire industries, such as the steel and automobile industries, where employment has been declining. Under those circumstances, expenditures for retiree health benefits increase substantially relative to total payroll, because the retiree health costs are spread over a smaller number of current employees. The study raises questions regarding the viability of unfunded retiree health plans in those firms where employment is continually declining.

Funding

Once employers have recognized the true nature of their retiree health liabilities and appreciate the likelihood that FASB could force them to take steps to finance these benefits through accrual of the liability during active employment, there may be growing interest in determining ways that the corporation can set aside funds in a trust to meet these obligations.

This study illustrates that the standard funding procedures used for pension plans can be used by corporations to fund their retiree health benefits, and also examines some modified funding approaches that deal with the relationship between trends in medical care costs and interest rates. For an employer considering funding of retiree health benefits, the study offers a comparative basis for assessing the effects of using alternative actuarial methods and the impact that different methods will have on annual employer costs.

Funding is also of interest to public policymakers and to organizations representing workers and retirees because funding affects the security of the benefit promise. As stated earlier, virtually all companies finance retiree health benefits on a pay-as-you-go basis. For pension plans, the federal government decided—in landmark legislation known as the Employee Retirement Income Security Act (ERISA)—that benefit security is enhanced by the advance funding of benefits. When measured against that ERISA standard, the retiree health promises made to retirees—estimated by EBRI at $60 billion for obligations to private-sector current retirees and $85 billion for private- and public-sector current retirees—are at risk.

For those interested in enhancing the security of retiree health benefits, this study illustrates how one measure of security—the ratio of funding to liabilities—is affected by the choice of different funding methods. In all cases, the use of advance funding can result in a higher level of benefit security.

When viewed in this context, the study also shows how current public policy discourages benefit security. Current law severely restricts tax incentives for funding and further restricts the ability to take into consideration, when funding, the future effects on liabilities resulting from increases in medical care costs. The tables in this study dramatize how the offer of what is, in effect, a benefit indexed to inflation, without funding to reflect that inflation, results in far less benefit security than if funding were allowed to take future health care cost increases into account. For example, the projections in this study for the unprojected method of funding show that, for most groups, at no point in time does the accumulated fund equal the accrued liabilities for workers then retired. There are major differences in advance funding a pension plan—

where future cost increases can be taken into account in the funding—versus advance funding a retiree health benefit, where the law prohibits it.

Benefit security of retiree health benefits will likely become a more prominent public policy issue. This study illustrates how increases in the number of a company's retirees can quickly and substantially magnify the financial obligation. When one considers the aging of the U.S. population and the continuing trend toward early retirement and compares that to the increase in costs resulting from an increased number of retirees, one realizes that total costs in the U.S. economy will go up significantly, if not skyrocket.

Finally, these concerns about benefit security are not only important for corporations and public policy: they are real-life, practical concerns of the millions of retirees, particularly early retirees, who depend on these employer-sponsored retiree health plans for coverage of needed medical services. The more this liability grows without funding behind it to secure the promise, the more retiree families are at risk of losing a major source of retirement income and health protection.

In conclusion, this study allows employers, policymakers, and others concerned about retiree health benefits to begin to consider: (1) the order of magnitude of corporate liabilities for this purpose; and (2) decisions about what type of funding, if any, would be compatible with the corporation's financial situation and desirable to encourage from a public-policy, benefit-security standpoint.

FRANK B. MCARDLE
Director, Education and Communications
Employee Benefit Research Institute

November 1987

Dedication

This study was undertaken as a memorial to Wendell A. Milliman, founder of Milliman & Robertson, Inc., one of the nation's largest actuarial consulting firms, and contributed to EBRI by Milliman & Robertson in his memory.

Wendell was 70 at his death in 1976. A 1926 graduate of the University of Washington, he was first employed as an actuarial trainee by Standard of Oregon. In 1928 he became actuary of Northwestern Life of Seattle and later served as actuary of the Seattle Employees' Retirement System. In 1929 he joined the Equitable Life Assurance Society where he advanced to second vice president.

Returning to Seattle in 1947, Wendell opened a one-man consulting office which subsequently led to the formation of Milliman & Robertson, Inc., which now employs more than 200 actuaries in 21 cities. From 1950 to 1955, he served as vice president of New York Life, organizing that company's initial entry into the field of group insurance.

Wendell was a former president of the Society of Actuaries. He helped form the American Academy of Actuaries and served as president of that organization in 1968. He was the author of numerous articles on health insurance, group insurance, and pensions, and participated in many of the developments in these fields. Wendell was an organizer and the second chairman of the Health Insurance Council and helped establish the Health Insurance Association of America.

"Wendell always felt that the actuary would have a major role in the health insurance field," notes James A. Curtis, F.S.A., chairman and chief executive officer of Milliman & Robertson, Inc. "Initially, his theory may not have been universal, because there were many who felt that premiums were merely a function of the cost, and that it didn't take an actuary to be able to divide the total cost by the number of policyholders. Now actuaries are found everywhere in the delivery of health care services. Wendell summed up the actuary's role some years ago when it appeared that national health insurance would be upon us and maybe consulting actuaries would not have a role. He stated, 'As long as there is a probability, there is a place for an actuary.' All of us at Milliman & Robertson are very proud of our heritage and the strong influence by our founders like Wendell. It is a real honor for us to be involved in this important study."

About the Authors

Phyllis A. Doran

Phyllis A. Doran is a consulting actuary in Milliman & Robertson's Washington, DC, office, where she manages that office's health benefits consulting practice. She is a Fellow of the Society of Actuaries and a member of the Society's Board of Governors. She has experience in all aspects of the financial management of group medical benefit plans, and is a frequent speaker on the subject.

Kenneth D. MacBain

Kenneth D. MacBain is a consulting actuary in the Philadelphia office of Milliman & Robertson, Inc., specializing in pension benefits. He is a Fellow of the Society of Actuaries and an Enrolled Actuary. He has worked extensively with pension and executive benefit plans, and also has experience with retiree medical benefits programs.

William A. Reimert

William A. Reimert is a consulting actuary in Milliman & Robertson's Philadelphia office, where he manages that office's pension practice. He is a Fellow of the Society of Actuaries and an Enrolled Actuary. He has extensive experience in the pension field, and is a frequent speaker on pension and employee benefits topics. He also authored the study note on pension plan terminations for the Joint Board for the Enrollment of Actuaries.

Executive Summary

Employer-sponsored retiree medical benefit programs are extremely important to retirees—and especially to the growing number of individuals who retire before age 65 and are not yet eligible for Medicare. These employer-sponsored programs also raise difficult financial and social issues. Government policymakers, mindful of the budget deficit, shy away from offering incentives to fund the benefit.

Very few companies either set aside funds in advance for payment of retiree medical benefits in future years or recognize liabilities for future benefit payments on their balance sheets. Employers, facing the possibility of huge liabilities for the programs, seek to control costs and limit legal liability, while still trying to offer meaningful benefits. And employees are concerned with the security of the benefits, particularly in view of recent cases of large employers discontinuing these benefits after filing for bankruptcy.

Background

A large number of employers provide medical benefits to their retirees, paid for in part or in full by the employer. In 1986, 76 percent of full-time health plan participants in medium and large establishments had coverage continued after early retirement; 90 percent of these had coverage continued after age 65.

Current Status

Factors contributing to the lack of advance funding or accrual accounting of these retiree medical benefits include the following.

Limited Understanding of Ultimate Costs—When retiree medical plans were first initiated by employers, generally as an extension of their plans for active employees, the associated costs were often considered immaterial. At that time, prior to the passage of the Employee Retirement Income Security Act (ERISA) in 1974, standards had not been adopted for vesting and funding of pension benefits; application of these concepts to medical benefits was not discussed. Therefore, employers tended to view these new benefits on a current-year cost basis rather than to look at the ultimate costs for providing benefits on a lifetime basis. Also, since medical benefits for active employees are usually funded on a pay-as-you-go basis, the same method seemed appropriate for retiree medical benefits.

Only recently has attention been focused on the long-term costs of retiree medical plans, and even today many employers do not fully understand their financial implications.

Uncertain Legal Status of the Employer Obligation—Many sponsors of retiree medical plans have informed their retirees and employees that these benefits are subject to modification or elimination at the company's discretion; many have also made benefit changes from time to time. Judicial rulings in recent years, however, have raised questions regarding an employer's legal ability to reduce these benefits, particularly for existing retirees.[1] In the climate of uncertainty created by these rulings, employers are hesitant to make major changes in their programs or take steps that might limit their flexibility to make future changes.

Accounting Standards—General practice has been to account for retiree medical benefits on a pay-as-you-go basis. The possibility of accruing the costs of these programs during the working lives of the covered employees was first addressed in writing by the Financial Accounting Standards Board (FASB) in 1982.[2] (FASB is the independent, nongovernmental authority for establishing accounting principles in the United States.) Since then, FASB has been studying the subject of accounting for postretirement medical and other benefits, and is scheduled to develop standards in this area.

Restrictions on Tax-Deductibility of Advance Funding Contributions—Current Internal Revenue Service (IRS) regulations allow some degree of tax-deductible advance funding of retiree medical benefits through Internal Revenue Code section 401(h) accounts, or through voluntary employee beneficiary associations (VEBAs) formed under section 419. Statutory limitations on these approaches prevent most employers from being able to fully fund their programs through these vehicles. Without the advantage of tax deductibility, competing uses for employer funds are generally more attractive than advance funding of benefit accounts.

Increasing Costs—For most employers, costs of retiree medical benefits on a pay-as-you-go basis have been increasing substantially. The

---

[1] Deborah J. Chollet and Robert B. Friedland, "Employer-Paid Retiree Health Insurance: History and Prospects for Growth," in Frank B. McArdle, ed., *The Changing Health Care Market* (Washington, DC: Employee Benefit Research Institute, 1987).

[2] Financial Accounting Standards Board, *Preliminary Views of the Financial Accounting Standards Board on Major Issues Related to Employers' Accounting for Pensions and Other Postemployment Benefits* (Washington, DC: Financial Accounting Standards Board, November 1982).

additional costs associated with advance funding could create a level of costs that would be unacceptable to some employers.

The growing awareness of these benefits, the current deliberations of FASB, and the uncertain legal climate surrounding postretirement medical plans are now leading many companies to take a closer look at their current programs. Many employers face significantly rising costs due to past promises for these benefits. Growing retiree populations, the rapid escalation of health care costs, and the shifting of Medicare costs to retirees and employers have contributed to an acceleration in the growth of costs for retiree health programs. Thus, there is increasing interest among employers in projecting future costs and liabilities, and in evaluating the potential impact of future accounting or funding standards. As a result, some companies are beginning to reduce the level of benefits offered to future generations of retirees and to increase retiree cost sharing.

Advance Funding Considerations

Concerns regarding the security of retiree medical benefits have begun to increase. As a result of such concern, the Deficit Reduction Act of 1984 (DEFRA) directed the Secretary of the Treasury to study the possible means of providing minimum standards for employee participation, vesting, accrual, and funding under welfare benefit plans for current and retired employees.

Recent bankruptcy cases in which retirees have lost medical benefits have led to discussion of ERISA-type funding and vesting standards for these plans. There are similarities between retiree medical and pension plans that lead some observers to conclude that an extension of ERISA to retiree medical plans would bring a necessary degree of benefit security.

There are, however, some major differences between retiree medical benefits and pension plans. These differences, outlined below, have implications for advance funding and should be addressed in any discussion of this issue.

Effects of External Factors on Costs of Medical Benefits—Costs of retiree medical benefits depend on the future costs of health care, changes in health care delivery and utilization patterns, and, perhaps, future breakthroughs in medical science. Further, the costs of most employer-provided programs are directly affected by changes in Medicare benefits or payment levels. The pattern of future costs is very sensitive to all of these factors, which are not readily controlled by the employer and are difficult to predict. In particular, the prospect of Medicare becoming a secondary payer for all retirees with employer-sponsored retiree health plans concerns many employers, even though no such legislation has ever been introduced.

Need for Flexibility in Benefit Guarantees—The typical plan of medical benefits tends to change over time in response to changes in medical costs and services. Thus, it is difficult to specify today a benefit promise appropriate for the medical care practices of 10 or 20 years from now or to guarantee a benefit in terms of the coverage provided. Many employers, concerned over the need to modify future benefits in order to control plan costs and adjust for changing medical care practices, may choose not to provide these benefits if forced to guarantee a specific level of coverage for long-term periods.

Lack of Generally Accepted Approaches to Accrual and Vesting of Retiree Medical Benefits—The typical current practice is to provide these benefits to employees that retire directly from the company (sometimes with a stricter service requirement than that applicable to regular pension benefits). Thus, "vesting"—the earning of a nonforfeitable right to a benefit—tends to occur at retirement or at eligibility for retirement. Under most plans, a long-service employee that leaves the company prior to eligibility for retirement does not have a vested interest in any postretirement medical benefits. Issues related to the vesting of these benefits have been the subject of several recent court rulings. Still, there are no definitive answers to such questions as:

(1) What are the vested rights of retirees receiving benefits? To what extent can an employer modify or eliminate medical benefits for retirees currently receiving them?

(2) What are the vested rights, if any, of current employees? Do those employees that are currently eligible to retire have the same rights to future medical benefits as existing retirees? What are the rights of other current employees with respect to these benefits?

While traditional pension funding techniques offer a starting point for exploring this subject, the factors outlined above complicate any discussion of funding postretirement medical benefits and must be addressed as part of any comprehensive study of this topic.

Summary and Major Findings

Potential solutions to the issues surrounding retiree medical programs must address a number of critical questions examined in this study:

(1) How high are the costs and liabilities undertaken when an employer promises retiree health benefits to its retirees and employees?
(2) What additional costs are involved in extending the benefits to the family members of current and future retirees?
(3) How sensitive are the projected costs to the current trends toward early retirement?
(4) To what extent are the costs affected by increases in the cost of medical care, which typically outpace changes in the general cost of living?
(5) How sensitive are projected costs and liabilities to the underlying demographic patterns for each particular employer and to the design of the retiree health benefit program itself?
(6) What are the cost-shifting implications of expected gradual curtailment in the level of coverage provided by Medicare?
(7) If advance funding of retiree medical benefits is required or permitted to a greater extent, what funding methods are appropriate, and what are the funding patterns under those methods? Should the approaches be different for accrual of costs for accounting purposes?
(8) Would an advance funding requirement enhance benefit security?
(9) Are there any reasonable ways to alter the manner in which retiree medical benefits are provided by employers, e.g., providing a defined level of contributions rather than a given level of coverage?

The analyses are based on three sample employee and retiree populations. Within this executive summary, the results are illustrated for only one of these hypothetical groups: a relatively stable population of 10,000 active employees plus approximately 1,600 current retirees, covered by a fairly modest plan ($500 deductible, 75 percent coinsurance, and $7,500 annual out-of-pocket limit).

Size of Liabilities

Based on one of several possible scenarios of trends in medical costs, the present value of benefits provided to this group is illustrated in table 1.

The total liability under this sample plan is allocated among current and future retirees and their spouses as illustrated in table 2.

Comparable values for a given population of retirees will vary, depending on the group's age composition, the number of spouses and extent of spousal coverage, the medical care utilization patterns of the group, and the level of benefits provided.

Medical Cost Trends

The trend in medical care costs has a significant impact on the size of projected benefit liabilities. During the last several decades, the

TABLE 1
Present Value of Retiree Health Benefits, Sample Plan

Covered Population	Total	Per Person
Current retirees	$24 million	$15,100 per retiree
Current employees		
coverage before age 65	15 million	1,500 per employee
coverage after age 65	55 million	5,500 per employee
total	70 million	7,000 per employee
Total	94 million	9,400 per employee

increase, or trend, in medical care costs has significantly exceeded the general rate of inflation. In recent years, for example, while the Consumer Price Index (CPI) varied between 2 and 4 percent, increases in medical care costs have ranged from 7 to 15 percent.

The current growth rate of medical care costs relative to general inflation is not likely to continue indefinitely because of practical limitations on the proportion of total national resources, measured by the Gross National Product (GNP), that can be spent on medical care. If GNP grows at a steady 5 percent and trends in medical costs at 10 percent per year, the result would be that, in the year 2035, medical services would represent 100 percent of GNP!

There is considerable uncertainty, however, regarding just what proportion of GNP may ultimately be allocated to medical care—and, correspondingly, how long medical care costs may continue to grow faster than the GNP or the rate of inflation. Therefore, this study uses three alternative medical care trend scenarios.

The "low," "medium," and "high" trend scenarios each start with annual medical care cost increases of 10 percent (the approximate

TABLE 2
Allocation of Total Liability, Sample Plan

Covered Population	Total	Per Employee
Retirees and employees	$54 million	$5,400
Spouses	40 million	4,000
Total	94 million	9,400

TABLE 3
Variation in Liabilities by Trend Scenario

Liability	Trend Scenario		
	Low	Medium	High
Present value of retirees' benefits, per retiree	$13,900	$15,100	$15,700
Present value of employees' benefits, per employee	5,600	7,000	8,300
Total present value of benefits, per employee	7,800	9,400	10,800
Ultimate level of the medical care component of GNP[a]	17%	22%	29%

[a]Gross National Product.

level during recent years) and decrease gradually to a 5 percent annual rate of increase (the assumed long-term growth rate in per capita GNP); this decline occurs over periods of 15, 25, and 35 years, respectively. For the sample groups, the "medium" trend scenario can be approximated by an 8 percent level annual rate of trend.

The present value of benefits based on all three trend scenarios is summarized in table 3—again, for the hypothetical employer group described above.

Sensitivity to Other Factors
These health benefit liabilities are sensitive to other key variables, summarized in table 4.

Medicare Changes
The erosion in the level of Medicare Part B charges that are recognized as "reasonable" has resulted in a reduction in the proportion of retiree medical costs funded by Medicare and a corresponding increase in the proportion funded by the employer's plan. If this trend continues, or, alternatively, if Medicare becomes secondary to employer plans, the liabilities under employer plans will increase substantially. For example, if the proportion of benefits covered by Medicare were to decline by 0.3 percent per year for 20 years, it would result in a 15 percent increase in the present value of benefits paid under this hypothetical plan. If Medicare were to become secondary to the employer plan, it would result in a 235 percent increase in the present value of benefits.

TABLE 4
Change in Employer Retiree Health Liabilities As Result of Changes in Key Variables, Based on Current Employees

Variable	Percent Change
Double the rate of early retirement	11%
Increase life expectancy by 1 year	6
Eliminate pre-65 coverage	−22
Increase percentage of spouse coverage payable under other plans from 10% to 20%	−5
Extend coverage of plan: $100 deductible, 80% coinsurance, $500 annual out-of-pocket limit	100
Require retirees to contribute 25% of total cost	−25
For plan requiring 25% contribution from retiree, freeze amount of retiree contribution at time of retirement	20

Prefunding Techniques and Costs

Retiree medical benefits are not generally funded during an employee's working years for various reasons, including the lack of adequate tax incentives. However, there is considerable discussion of the possibility of imposing requirements for employer advance funding of these benefits before retirement.

The cost of funding retiree medical benefits is calculated in this study based on projections of future employee populations for the sample groups. Advance funding methods borrowed from pension practice are compared with current "pay-as-you-go" procedures. These methods produce the annual funding requirements presented in table 5. In this illustration, advance funding costs continue to exceed pay-as-you-go costs even after 50 years for a stable or growing employee population.

If a company were to decline in size, advance funding costs would tend to drop below pay-as-you-go costs. Under such circumstances, pay-as-you-go costs may exceed corporate resources, forcing reductions in retiree benefits. Advance funding costs, on the other hand, would decline at approximately the same rate as the group of active employees, and benefits would be provided to retirees from accumulated funds.

TABLE 5
Cost of Funding Retiree Medical Benefits

		Pension Funding Methods		
Year	Pay-As-You-Go	Projected Unit Credit	Entry-Age Normal	Aggregate
		annual contribution per active employee		
0	$ 200	$1,100	$1,400	$1,500
10	300	1,500	1,700	1,600
20	800	1,500	1,600	1,500
30	1,500	1,700	1,800	1,500
40	2,600	2,700	3,000	2,800
50	4,300	4,400	4,900	4,700
		fund (millions)		
0	$0	$ 0	$ 0	$ 0
10	0	154	192	193
20	0	375	426	426
30	0	617	668	667
40	0	1,243	1,331	1,273
50	0	2,470	2,649	2,482

Because of the uncertainty of future medical trends, a number of modified advance funding methods have been proposed in other studies of retiree medical benefits. Two of these methods—the Unprojected Unit Credit (No Trend) and Unit Credit with No Trend or Discount Rate—are examined in this study, along with a third method, Projected Unit Credit with Trend Equal to Per Capita GNP Growth Rate. These modified funding methods produce generally lower annual funding costs than full funding methods but higher costs than pay-as-you-go. At year 50, the Unprojected Unit Credit method produces a fund only one-third the size of that produced by using the Projected Unit Credit method.

Benefit Security

The funds developed under the full funding methods generally are sufficient to cover the benefits of existing retirees in five years and future benefits for vested employees (i.e., those eligible to retire) in five to ten years. These funds, however, generally do not reach 100 percent of total accrued benefits for all retirees and employees but stabilize slightly below that level.

Modified advance funding methods generally accumulate funds more slowly; in fact, the Unprojected Unit Credit method does not even produce sufficient assets to cover 100 percent of benefits for existing retirees.

In the event of cessation of employer operations, the liabilities for employees eligible to retire increase, since these employees will retire at once. Under these circumstances, funds will not go as far in covering the accrued benefits of all employees.

Study Objectives and Methodology

In this study, actuarial techniques are used to analyze advance funding and expensing of retiree medical benefits. Using several model groups, the study estimates the benefit liabilities and examines alternative funding methods under several economic scenarios. In addition, the effects of changes in benefits and possible future policy changes are measured.

The model groups have been chosen to cover a range of employer characteristics (see description below). However, it is not possible to demonstrate the effects of the methods shown under all possible conditions; the samples shown should be considered as illustrations only.

This study provides a framework for evaluating various assumptions and techniques—including some that may not be directly addressed here. The inclusion of any particular assumption or technique does not imply that it is preferable to another; rather, those included have been selected to illustrate a range of possibilities.

Description of Model Groups

Three hypothetical groups form the basis for the calculation of all values presented in this study. The groups were selected from among those presented in *Pension Cost Method Analysis*, a study published by the American Academy of Actuaries Committee on Pension Actuarial Principles and Practices.[3] The Academy study includes population characteristics and projection assumptions for 10 model groups, which are identified as groups A through J. The following groups were selected for use in this study because of their differences in maturity, turnover, and size of retiree population.

> **Group A: Stable**—This represents a reasonably mature and stable group that is projected to continue to grow. It is typical of many large companies.

---

[3]Committee on Pension Actuarial Principles and Practices, American Academy of Actuaries, *Pension Cost Method Analysis* (Washington, DC: American Academy of Actuaries, 1985).

TABLE 6
Major Characteristics of Model Groups

Characteristics	Group A (stable)	Group F (older)	Group H (new)
Number of employees	10,000	10,000	10,000
average age	36	39	39
average years of service	7	11	4
Number of retirees			
under age 65	604	1,152	0
over age 65	984	1,880	14
total	1,588	3,032	14

Group F: Older, Declining—This represents an older, mature group that is gradually declining. Turnover is high at all ages and durations of employment.

Group H: New—This represents a group formed five years ago with a high average age at employment and relatively high turnover.

Each group has a total of 10,000 active employees initially. Table 6 summarizes the major characteristics of each group. The assumptions used in projecting future populations of these groups are those presented in the Academy study, with a few exceptions (summarized in appendix A).

Study Methodology

This study uses two types of projections:

(1) Closed group projections involve projections of the current population of employees and retirees for each group, without consideration of new hires in future years. Closed group projections are used to derive liability values based on the group as it exists today. Closed group values are useful for testing the effects of changes in benefits or assumptions. In addition, measurements of current accrued and/or vested benefit liabilities, however defined, are based on projections of the closed group.

The values presented in Part One are based on closed group projections.

(2) Open group projections include assumptions regarding future entrants, or new hires. This approach is used to analyze the fund that develops over a period of several years under an advance funding approach.

Part Two presents the results of 50-year open group projections for groups A, F, and H. In these projections, the number of new entrants in each year is based on the annual growth assumption of the group, as presented in table 7.

TABLE 7
Annual Projected Growth Rates

Group	Rate
A (stable)	2%
F (older)	−2%, −7%
H (new)	2%

Group F is projected under two assumptions: a 2 percent annual rate of decline and a 7 percent rate of decline. The latter projection illustrates the effects of funding on a rapidly declining group; at a 7 percent annual rate of decline, Group F reduces to one-half its original size in 10 years.

Chapters VII and VIII analyze the fund buildup that occurs over 50 years for each of these groups under a range of funding methods and economic scenarios.

Issues Not Covered in This Study

This study is focused primarily on the measurement and funding issues surrounding retiree medical plans. Additional issues, also relevant and important in evaluating retiree medical programs in the U.S., include

(1) legal framework for plans,

(2) impact on the U.S. economy if tax-sheltered funding is required, and

(3) possibility of an expanded program of government-provided benefits.

For a discussion of these and other issues, see the following EBRI publications:

Financing the Elderly's Health Care (forthcoming)
The Changing Health Care Market (1987)
Medicare Reform: The Private-Sector Impact (1985)
The Changing Profile of Pensions in America (1985)
Retirement Security and Tax Policy (1984)

Part One
Present Values of Future Benefits (Closed Group)

I. Present Value of Future Benefits— Basic Results

This chapter describes the basic model and summarizes the present value of future benefits under a given set of assumptions for each of the model groups. In particular, the economic assumptions that must be made to develop these values have a significant effect on the results; a discussion of these assumptions is also included. All calculations in this chapter, and those in chapters II, III, and IV, are based on "closed group" techniques—i.e., there is no provision for new entrants. "Closed group" calculations are common in pension funding and liability calculations; in fact, ERISA mandates closed group techniques for pension plan funding.

Development of Present Values of Future Benefits

The present value of future benefits (PVFB) is the value of all future benefits expected to be paid for a closed group population, discounted at an assumed interest rate. The PVFB represents the dollar amount needed today that, with future investment earnings, would be adequate to pay all future benefits as they become due.

Present values of future retiree medical benefits are developed as follows.

Projection of Covered Population by Year

The number of covered retirees and spouses, distributed by age and sex, are projected for each year in the future. The current employee and retiree population form the starting point; assumptions regarding turnover or separation, retirement, mortality, and probability of marriage at retirement are used to project future populations. Dependent child coverage is ignored in this study, so no assumptions regarding number of children are made.

Per Capita Plan Costs

All values are based on assumed annual per capita medical plan costs. The per capita cost varies by age of the covered retiree or spouse. It represents the average cost of the medical benefits program per covered person, whether expressed as an insurance premium or as the total claims incurred, including an allowance for administrative costs. First-year per capita costs are the same in each projection;

TABLE I.1
Assumed Average First-Year Per Capita Plan Costs

Age	Single Retiree	Married Retiree
60	$880	$1,680
70	280	540

costs in future years depend on the assumed annual increase in plan costs, or trend (discussed later). The per capita plan costs used for sample ages in this study are shown in table I.1. These costs are representative of those of many programs in place today.

Actual employer program costs vary widely, depending on the age distribution of the covered population, the benefit coverage, utilization patterns, retiree cost sharing and other factors; many are significantly higher or lower than those assumed here. Chapter III presents sample plan costs for a range of benefit plans. The first-year plan costs shown above resemble those of a fairly low benefit plan ($500 deductible, 75 percent coinsurance, $7,500 annual out-of-pocket limit). For certain levels of coverage, per capita plan costs could be two to three times as high as those presented in table I.1.

The present values of future benefits presented in this study vary in proportion to any differences in the assumed first-year per capita costs.

Total Plan Costs by Year

Total plan costs in each year are derived by applying the projected population counts, by age, to the corresponding per capita plan costs, by age, for that year.

Present Value of Future Benefits

In this study, closed-group projection results are expressed as the present value of future benefits (PVFB). To repeat, the PVFB is the discounted value of all future plan costs by year, based on an assumed discount rate.

Present Value of Future Benefits for Model Groups

This section presents sample benefit values for the three model groups used in the study. These values are based on closed-group projections, using the method outlined above. The major assumptions used in these projections are outlined in table I.2.

TABLE I.2
Major Projection Assumptions

	Group A (stable)	Group F (older)	Group H (new)
Average annual trend in plan costs = 8%.			
Discount rate = 7%.			
Ultimate rates of separation and disability— sample rates per 1,000			
age 40	62	131	16
age 50	24	85	3
age 60	16	14	12
Retirement—sample rates per 1,000			
age 55	30	50	30
age 57	30	50	30
age 60	100	100	30
age 62	150	250	100
age 65	1,000	1,000	1,000

Eligibility for benefits:
- Age 55 with 10 years of service, or age 65 regardless of service.
- Spouse is covered.
- Surviving spouse of a covered retiree is covered.

Percentage of retirees with spouses at time of retirement: 70 percent
Percentage of spouse benefits payable by other medical plans: 10 percent

The values presented here are based on an 8 percent average annual medical care trend assumption and a 7 percent discount rate (see discussion of economic assumptions below). As shown in chapter II, these values will vary significantly if different trend/discount-rate combinations are assumed; those shown here are illustrative only. These assumptions were selected to approximate the medium trend scenarios set forth in the following section.

Table I.3 summarizes annual benefit payments and the present values of future benefits for all current retirees and employees in each group; the present values are also shown on a per retiree or per employee basis. Values for current employees are shown separately for benefits in effect from retirement up to age 65 and benefits in effect after reaching age 65; those over age 65 reflect the effect of Medicare coverage. All values include the costs of spouse coverage, including surviving spouses of deceased retirees.

TABLE I.3
Present Value of Future Benefits and Current Payments[a] (millions)

Benefits	Group A (stable)	Group F (older)	Group H (new)
Current-year benefit payments	$ 2	$ 3	$ 0
Present value of future benefits			
current retirees	24	43	0
current employees			
coverage under age 65	15	14	22
coverage over age 65	55	44	95
total employees	70	58	117
total current retirees			
and employees	94	101	117
Present value of benefits per person			
per current retiree	15,100	14,200	—
per current employee			
coverage under age 65	1,500	1,400	2,200
coverage over age 65	5,500	4,400	9,500
total per current employee	7,000	5,800	11,700
total current retirees			
and employees	9,400	10,100	11,700

[a] All values include spouse coverage.

The allocation of the present values of future benefits among retirees and employees and their spouses is presented in table I.4.

Discussion of Economic Assumptions

Trend

A projection of retiree medical benefits for future periods requires an assumption as to the future trend in medical costs. "Trend" refers to the annual rate of change in per capita plan costs due to factors other than changes in the group's composition by age or marital status. As such, the trend is affected by such factors as medical care inflation, changes in medical care utilization or delivery patterns, and changes in the health status of the covered population.

Projected future benefit costs depend heavily on the medical care trends assumed; however, it is impossible to predict these trends over

TABLE I.4
Allocation of Present Value of Future Benefits (millions)

	Group A (stable)	Group F (older)	Group H (new)
Present value of future benefits			
current retirees			
retirees	$ 13	$ 24	$ 0
spouses	11	19	0
total	24	43	0
current employees			
employees	41	34	69
spouses	29	24	48
total	70	58	117
total			
retirees and employees	54	58	69
spouses	40	43	48
total	94	101	117
Present value of benefits per person			
current retirees		per retiree	
retirees	8,200	7,900	—
spouses	6,900	6,300	—
total	15,100	14,200	—
current employees		per employee	
employees	4,100	3,400	6,900
spouses	2,900	2,400	4,800
total	7,000	5,800	11,700
total		per employee	
retirees and employees	5,400	5,800	6,900
spouses	4,000	4,300	4,800
total	9,400	10,100	11,700

a long period with certainty. This means that projections of future plan costs are subject to significant variability.

In this study, trend represents the increase in total medical costs as if no deductible or out-of-pocket maximum were applied. In practice, if there is a deductible and it is not increased to keep up with medical cost trends, the trend in plan costs will be higher than the medical cost trend. This is because the deductible has the effect of "leveraging" the impact of trend on costs exceeding the deductible. The approach used in this study, then, in effect assumes that employers will increase deductibles and out-of-pocket maximums over time at a rate consistent with total medical cost increases, and that no such leveraging will occur.

Discount Rate

The present value of future benefits is calculated by applying a discount rate to each future year's benefit cost. This discount factor is based on an assumed interest rate, compounded annually; each year's benefit cost is divided by this compound interest factor. Thus, a high trend assumption will increase future benefit costs, while a high discount rate will decrease the present value of those benefits.

Relationship of Trend and Discount Rate to GNP Growth

The present value of future benefits for closed groups, therefore, depends on the difference between the average trend and the discount rate, rather than on their absolute levels. Because the long-term behavior of these two economic factors is not independent, it is useful to consider the difference (or spread) between the average trend and the discount rate. This spread is subject to some broad constraints over the long term that do not apply to the individual values.

Actuaries have traditionally assumed that interest rates are a composite of a real rate of return (of perhaps 3 to 4 percent per year) plus the rate of expected inflation. A similar approach is utilized by economists in analyzing growth in the Gross National Product (GNP): the effect of inflation is subtracted from total GNP growth, by utilizing the GNP deflator, to derive the real rate of growth in GNP. This real rate of growth can then be adjusted for changes in population to derive the rate of growth in per capita GNP.

Assuming that the long-term real rate of growth in per capita GNP is fairly stable (at about 1.5 percent per year), it is possible to establish a relationship between total GNP growth and a given rate of interest (i.e., discount rate). For example:

   interest rate = general rate of inflation + 3.5 percent

   rate of growth in per capita GNP = general rate of inflation + 1.5 percent

Therefore,

   rate of growth in per capita GNP = interest rate − 2 percent

The actual values shown above are subject to variation; however, these values should remain within a fairly small range, which means that there is a general level of long-term predictability regarding the relationship between interest rates and per capita growth in GNP.

It is also possible to establish a link between medical trend and the growth in GNP. Average rates of medical trend have exceeded the rate of growth in per capita GNP by a substantial margin (5 to 10 percent per year) over the past 20 years. This, however, is unlikely to continue indefinitely, due to the continuously increasing share of GNP that is consumed by medical care when such margins develop.

Medical care spending has now increased to more than 11 percent of the total GNP of the U.S. economy. If the medical care component of GNP were to grow at, say, 10 percent per year while total GNP grew at 5 percent annually for years to come, the medical care component of GNP would increase in the future as follows.

Year	Medical Care Services As a Percentage of GNP
1985	11%
1995	18
2005	28
2015	44
2025	71

By the year 2035, the entire GNP would be medical care services! This illustration points out the degree to which the current spread between the medical trend and growth in per capita GNP can be expected to decline in the future. We believe it is reasonable to assume that medical care is not likely to grow to more than 25 or 30 percent of GNP.

Thus, since there is a likely long-term relationship between medical trend and growth in per capita GNP, and between interest rates and growth in per capita GNP, the medical trend and interest rate used to derive present values should be based on the same assumed underlying rate of growth in per capita GNP.

Most of the closed-group benefit values shown in this report are based on a 7 percent discount rate. The average trend assumption of a level 8 percent by year has been chosen as a simplifying representation of a varying trend pattern. As shown in chapter VI, an estimate of future trends might actually be represented by a series of declining rates by calendar year. In that chapter, three such series, or trend scenarios, are defined—referred to as low, medium, and high—as summarized below.

Annual Trend	Low	Medium	High
	\multicolumn{3}{c}{years}	
10%	1–3	1–5	1–7
9	4–6	6–10	8–14
8	7–9	11–15	15–21
7	10–12	16–20	22–28
6	13–15	21–25	29–35
5	16+	26+	36+

Under these low, medium, and high trend scenarios, the medical care component of GNP would ultimately grow to 17, 22, or 29 percent, respectively.

The level 8 percent trend rate assumed in this chapter represents a reasonable approximation of the medium trend scenario for the closed-group benefit values. Table I.5 illustrates the range in benefit liabilities that is produced by the low, medium, and high trend scenarios defined above.

TABLE I.5
Variation in Present Value of Future Benefits by Trend Scenario (millions)

Covered Population	Group A (stable)	Group F (older)	Group H (new)
Current retirees			
low	$ 22	$ 39	$ 0
medium	24	43	0
high	25	45	0
Current employees			
low	56	48	92
medium	70	58	117
high	83	66	143
Total current employees and retirees			
low	78	87	92
medium	94	101	117
high	108	111	143

II. Sensitivity of Benefit Values to Changes in Assumptions

This chapter examines the effects that certain changes in assumptions or circumstances will have on the benefit values of the model groups. The economic assumptions are the most critical, as a seemingly small change in these values may produce a significant change in benefit values; the effects of varying the trend assumption are illustrated.

In addition, the effects of changes in early retirement rates, mortality rates, eligibility provisions, reductions in coverage prior to age 65, and the degree of other coverage for spouses are illustrated.

Economic Assumptions

As discussed in chapter I, it is the difference, or spread, between the assumed average trend and the discount rate, rather than their absolute values, that affects the present value of benefits. For example, the following sets of assumptions will produce roughly equivalent present values.

Average Trend	Discount Rate	Spread
8%	7%	1%
11	10	1
5	4	1

In all of these cases, the trend is one percentage point higher than the discount rate. However, if the discount rate remains at 7 percent and the average trend is changed, the resulting present values may vary substantially.

This is illustrated in table II.1. The effects of changing from an 8 percent average trend while maintaining a 7 percent discount rate are shown for the model groups. For example, if the average trend is increased from 8 percent to 9 percent, the total present value of future benefits can be expected to increase by 10 to 40 percent, depending on the proportion of the covered group that is currently retired.

Early Retirement Rates

If early retirement rates are doubled at all ages for the model groups, the present value of future benefits is increased 11 percent

TABLE II.1
Percent Change in Present Value of Future Benefits Due to Change in Average Trend[a]

		Retirees Only			Retirees and Employees		
Average Trend	Spread[b]	Group A (stable)	Group F (older)	Group H (new)	Group A (stable)	Group F (older)	Group H (new)
5%	−2%	−25%	−26%	−28%	−48%	−37%	−60%
7	0	−10	−10	−11	−21	−15	−27
8	1	0	0	0	0	0	0
9	2	13	12	13	29	20	39
11	4	41	43	45	129	80	183
13	6	85	90	91	340	189	507

[a]Discount rate = 7%; base trend = 8%.
[b]The spread is the difference between the rate of average trend and the discount rate. Note that the term "spread" in pension valuation assumptions is usually associated with the difference between the discount rate and the salary scale.

overall; the value of benefits received prior to age 65 is increased about 50 percent. These results are summarized in table II.2. The present values that result from this change would apply to groups with early retirement rates twice as high as those of the model groups.

TABLE II.2
Effect of Doubling Early Retirement Rates on the Present Value of Future Benefits (PVFB) for Current Employees

	Group A (stable)	Group F (older)	Group H (new)
Average retirement age			
basic early retirement rates	62.6	61.8	63.2
doubled early retirement rates	60.9	59.9	61.8
Percent change in PVFB if early retirement rates are doubled			
coverage under age 65	51%	46%	54%
coverage at ages 65 and over	0	0	0
total	11	11	11

TABLE II.3
Effect of Reducing Mortality Rates on Present Value of Future Benefits (PVFB) for Current and Retired Employees[a]

	Group A (stable)	Group F (older)	Group H (new)
Percent change in PVFB	6%	5%	6%

[a]Reduction is equivalent to a one-year increase in life expectancy at birth.

Mortality

If mortality rates are reduced by an amount equivalent to approximately a one-year increase in total life expectancy at birth, the present value of future benefits for the model groups is increased by about 6 percent. Over the past 20 years, life expectancy in the U.S. at birth has increased by one year approximately every five years.

Table II.3 summarizes these results. The one-year increase in life expectancy is accomplished by reducing mortality rates from 100 percent to 90 percent of the 1983 "Group Annuity Mortality Table" (GAM-83). GAM-83 is commonly used for pension plan valuations.

Eligibility for Early Retirement

Benefit values in this study are based on the assumption that benefits are paid to all employees that retire at age 55 or older with 10 years of service, or at age 65 regardless of length of service; employees

TABLE II.4
Effect of Five-Year Service Requirement on Present Value of Future Benefits (PVFB) for Current Employees

	Group A (stable)	Group F (older)	Group H (new)
Percent of employees hired at ages 45 and over	12%	9%	23%
Percent change in PVFB due to reduction in service requirement			
coverage under age 65	5	4	7
coverage at ages 65 and over	1	0	1
total	1	1	2

TABLE II.5
Effect of Reductions in Coverage Prior to Age 65 on Present Value of Future Benefits (PVFB) for Current Employees

	Group A (stable)	Group F (older)	Group H (new)
Percent change in PVFB due to reductions in coverage			
elimination of all coverage prior to age 65	−22%	−25%	−19%
50% retiree contribution required prior to age 65	−11	−12	−9

that terminate prior to meeting these requirements receive no benefits. Spouses of covered retirees also receive benefit coverage for life.

For the model groups, if the service requirement for age 55 retirement is changed from 10 years to 5, the total present value of future benefits is increased by about 1 percent. For benefits received prior to age 65, the present value is increased by about 5 percent. Table II.4 summarizes these results.

For these groups, only 9 percent to 23 percent of all employees are hired at ages 45 and older. Obviously, for groups with higher percentages of employees hired at these ages, the effect of a decrease in the 10-year service requirement could be substantially greater than 1 percent overall.

TABLE II.6
Effect of Increase in Other Coverage for Spouses on Present Value of Future Benefits (PVFB) for Current and Retired Employees

	Group A (stable)	Group F (older)	Group H (new)
Percent of employees married at time of retirement	71%	71%	70%
Percent change in PVFB due to higher frequency of other spouses' coverage:			
20% of spouses' benefit costs (rather than 10%) are payable under other coverage	−5	−5	−5

Reductions in Coverage Prior to Age 65

If coverage prior to age 65 were eliminated, the present value of future benefits for the model groups would decrease by about 20 percent to 25 percent. If a 50 percent contribution were required from retirees prior to age 65, the reduction would be about 10 percent. These results are summarized in table II.5. For groups with higher proportions of early retirements than these, the effects of the reductions would be greater.

Other Coverage for Spouses

The benefit values in this study reflect an assumption that 10 percent of eligible spouses' benefit costs are not payable due to the existence of other coverage. (If a spouse has coverage through his or her own employer, that coverage would be primary and would pay benefits first.) If this 10 percent assumption is increased to 20 percent, the present value of future benefits for the model groups is decreased by 5 percent. Table II.6 summarizes this result. For groups with a higher frequency of marriage at retirement, the effect of a change in the extent of other spouses' coverage would be greater.

III. Effects of Plan Design and Benefit Changes

This chapter discusses the effects of changes in plan design on benefit values for the model groups. Since values depend on the benefit plan in effect and future changes in benefits, both of these factors are discussed. In addition, the effects of freezing retiree contributions at retirement are illustrated, and effects of future changes in Medicare are considered.

Benefit Plan

The benefit costs presented in this study are based on representative first-year per capita plan costs for plans in effect today.

Actual plan costs vary significantly from employer to employer due to differences in coverage and claims experience. As an illustration of the general relationships among plan costs by level of coverage, table III.1 presents some sample ranges of per capita costs for three benefit plans. These cost levels are typical of many comprehensive major medical plans today.

The costs in this study resemble those for a fairly low level of benefits—$500 deductible, 75 percent coinsurance, and $7,500 annual out-of-pocket limit. Costs for richer plans could be two to three times as high as those in this study. Table III.2 summarizes the approximate

TABLE III.1
Illustrative Costs by Type of Benefit Plan

Level of Coverage	Sample Annual Per Capita Costs—1987	
	Age 60	Age 70[a]
$100 deductible, 80% coinsurance, $500 out-of-pocket limit	$1,500–2,000	$450–600
$250 deductible, 80% coinsurance, $2,500 out-of-pocket limit	1,250–1,750	350–500
$500 deductible, 75% coinsurance, $7,500 out-of-pocket limit	750–1,250	200–350

[a] Age 70 costs assume a Medicare carve-out plan (i.e., benefits otherwise payable are reduced by the dollar amount of benefits paid by Medicare).

TABLE III.2
Effect of Plan Changes on Present Value of Future Benefits (PVFB)

Benefit Level	Increase in PVFB over Values Shown in This Study
High	
$100 deductible, 80% coinsurance, $500 out-of-pocket limit	100%
Medium	
$250 deductible, 80% coinsurance, $2,500 out-of-pocket limit	50
Low	
$500 deductible, 75% coinsurance, $7,500 out-of-pocket limit	0

effect of changes in benefits on the present value of future benefits for the model groups, based on the relationships shown in table III.1.

Future Changes in Benefits

The annual trends used to project future benefits in this study are expressed in terms of an overall rate of increase in medical care costs. This implies that the proportion of benefits paid by the plan stays constant over time relative to total medical claims incurred. Similarly, this means that the percentage share paid by the employee and, for those over age 65, by Medicare also will remain constant over time.

In other words, if the benefit plan pays, for example, 60 percent of the average retiree's medical claims in the first year, then it is assumed that plan deductibles and out-of-pocket limits change over time so that the plan continues to pay 60 percent, even as inflation changes total medical costs. To the extent that the benefit coverage does not change in this manner, but becomes higher or lower than 60 percent over time, benefit values will differ.

There are two specific situations in which the assumption that a constant proportion of benefits will be covered is not valid: (1) when retiree contributions are frozen, in dollar terms, at retirement; or (2) when Medicare coverage changes.

TABLE III.3
Effect of Freeze in Retiree Contributions on Employer-Paid Present Value of Future Benefits (PVFB)

Retiree Contribution As Percent of Total Cost at Time of Retirement	Percent Change in PVFB Due to Contributions		Increase Due to Freeze
	Without freeze	With freeze	
10%	−10%	−4%	7%
25	−25	−10	20
50	−50	−20	60

Freeze in Retiree Contributions

If the retiree is required to contribute a percentage of the cost of medical coverage, the present value of future benefits payable by the employer is reduced. If the dollar amount of the retiree contribution is frozen, however, so that he or she pays the same dollar amount in all future years, the employer's costs are increased significantly over what they otherwise would be.

Table III.3 illustrates the effect of this freeze in retiree contributions for initial retiree contribution levels of 10 percent, 25 percent, and 50 percent. If, for example, the retiree is required to contribute 10 percent of the plan cost in all years, the employer's total cost would be reduced by this amount. On the other hand, if the retiree's contribution is set at 10 percent of the benefit cost when he or she retires, and then "frozen" at this same dollar amount in all future years of retirement, the employer's costs are reduced by only 4 percent. The employer's total costs are 7 percent higher with this freeze on retiree contributions than if the contribution were to increase each year for the retiree.

Changes in Medicare

The assumption in these projections that the benefit level stays constant relative to total medical claims incurred implies that the proportion of benefits covered by Medicare for persons over age 65 remains constant. This has not been true historically, however. Erosion in the level of Supplementary Medical Insurance (Part B) charges that are recognized by Medicare as "reasonable" has resulted in a reduction in the proportion of claims paid by Medicare under many employer plans.

The Part B deductible has remained at $75 since 1981. This has partially offset the effects of the erosion in "reasonable charge" levels because the percentage of Part B charges represented by $75 has

19

TABLE III.4
Effect of Decline in Medicare Coverage Levels on Present Value of Future Benefits (PVFB) for Current Employees[a]

Percent Change in PVFB	Group A (stable)	Group F (older)	Group H (new)
10-year decline			
coverage under age 65	0%	0%	0%
coverage at ages 65 and over	10	9	10
total	7	7	8
20-year decline			
coverage under age 65	0	0	0
coverage at ages 65 and over	19	18	20
total	15	14	16

[a] Assumes a 0.3 percent annual decline in proportion of benefits covered by Medicare for 10 years or 20 years, as indicated.

declined due to inflation. The Hospital Insurance (Part A) deductible has increased every year, roughly in proportion to increases in hospital costs. Overall, the proportion of benefit costs covered by Medicare under a typical employer plan has declined at a rate of roughly 0.3 percent per year in recent years.

The way in which changes in Medicare will affect employer plan costs depends on the method used to coordinate benefits with Medicare. Most employer-provided plans are considered "carve-outs." In the general concept of a carve-out approach, the benefit payment is determined in two steps. First, the benefit is calculated as if Medicare did not exist by applying the deductible and coinsurance provisions of the employer plan. Second, the amount actually paid by Medicare is subtracted, and the balance is paid to the retiree.

In practice, however, there are many variations in the way a carve-out works. There is no standardized definition of carve-out; the term is used to cover a range of approaches that could produce widely differing benefit payments in a given situation. For example, some plans coordinate with Medicare using the standard coordination of benefits (COB) clause; under this approach, the plan fills in Medicare deductibles and coinsurance up to a maximum benefit payment determined by the plan.

Because of the variations in the way a carve-out works, it is not possible to generalize as to the effects that changes in Medicare would have on an employer's carve-out plan costs. However, the costs in table III.4 illustrate the potential effects that Medicare changes can have.

Table III.4 shows the effect on the present value of future benefits if the proportion of benefit costs covered by Medicare declines at a rate of 0.3 percent per year for the next 10 to 20 years. This roughly corresponds to the recent history of Medicare coverage reductions. The relationships in table III.4 do not apply to a plan that pays benefits only up to Medicare "reasonable charge" levels; they do apply, however, to a typical Medicare carve-out or COB plan.

Larger cutbacks in Medicare benefits, such as increases in the relative levels of deductibles, could have significantly greater effects on benefit values. If Medicare were to immediately become secondary for employer-sponsored retiree medical plans (as it is for active employee coverage) so that all reductions for Medicare were eliminated, the total present value of future benefits for the sample groups would increase by more than 200 percent. Table III.5 summarizes the effect of such a change.

TABLE III.5
Effect on Present Value of Future Benefits (PVFB) for Current Employees If Medicare Coverage Becomes Secondary[a]

Coverage	Group A (stable)	Group F (older)	Group H (new)
Coverage under age 65	0%	0%	0%
Coverage at ages 65 and over	300	300	300
Total	234	226	244

[a] Assumes change is effective immediately and includes coverage for spouses.

IV. Accrual and Vesting of Benefits

The concepts of accrual and vesting of benefits during an employee's period of active service are well established for pension plans. "Accrual" refers to the rate at which benefits are earned. In pension plans, the rate of accrual is set forth in the plan provisions. Thus, the amount of the pension accrued by an employee at any point in time can be determined, based on these provisions. The extent to which the employee has a nonforfeitable right to these accrued benefits in the event of termination of employment prior to retirement is referred to as "vesting."

The method of accrual and the vesting schedule determine the benefit amount that an employee is entitled to receive when he or she leaves employment. An employee that is partially or fully vested and leaves employment before retirement age retains the vested portion of the accrued benefit and has the nonforfeitable right to receive that benefit upon reaching retirement age.

Under most retiree medical plans there is no concept of accrual, nor any formal vesting policy. Benefits could be said to accrue and vest at retirement or when an employee becomes eligible to retire. However, because the employer's obligation is often not clearly defined, these concepts are rarely applied to retiree medical benefits.

It is possible to apply an accrual concept to medical benefits if the focus is on the accrual of the employer's share of the total cost of the program. For example, consider a plan that requires employees to pay 20 percent of the cost of postretirement benefits through contributions, with the employer providing for the other 80 percent. Assume that 25 years of service are required to receive these benefits.

In this example, reduced benefits could be provided for fewer than 25 years of service by making a pro-rata reduction in the employer's share of the contribution, with the employee's share increased to make up the difference. For an employee with 10 years of service the benefit would be determined as follows:

maximum employer contribution × years of service to date/25
 = accrued employer contribution
80% × 10/25 = 32%

Thus,

employer's share = 32%
employee's share = 68%

Under this approach, benefits would be accrued ratably over 25 years.

Several accrual methods are possible for retiree medical benefits. Table IV.1 illustrates how benefits would accrue under each of the following methods for a hypothetical employee.

Alternative Accrual Methods

Accrual at Retirement
No benefits are accrued until the date of retirement. If an employee terminates prior to retirement, the accrued benefit is zero.

Accrual at Eligibility for Retirement
The benefits for each employee are accrued in full at the earliest date of eligibility for retirement. Thus, an employee could accrue the full benefit without actually retiring.

Ratable Accrual from Date of Hire to Age 65
Benefits begin accruing at date of hire. The total benefit is accrued ratably over the period from the employee's hire date to age 65. For example, an employee that was hired at age 25 would have accrued one-half of his or her benefit by age 45.

Ratable Accrual from Date of Hire to Earliest Eligibility for Retirement
Benefits begin accruing at the date of hire (as above) but are fully accrued at earliest eligibility for retirement.

Ratable Accrual over Fixed Period of Service
Benefits are accrued over a fixed period, such as 25 years. An employee that retires or terminates with less than the required period of service receives a proportionate amount of the benefit.

For the example shown in table IV.1, the benefit percentage accrued at age 50 ranges from 0 to 40 percent and, at age 65, from 64 to 80 percent.

For a given accrual method, it is necessary to define the nature of the benefit that is accruing. For example, if pro-rata accrual is applied to the full level of medical coverage available upon retirement, then in effect the benefit is fully indexed for future inflation. It would also be possible to accrue nonindexed benefits, or benefit levels based on the current costs of coverage without adjustment for future inflation.

Table IV.2 summarizes the accrued benefit liabilities produced for fully indexed benefits by the first four accrual methods above when

TABLE IV. 1
Illustration of Alternative Accrual Methods

Hypothetical plan provisions:
- For a fully accrued benefit, employer pays 80 percent of the cost of the retiree medical benefit; retiree pays remaining 20 percent.
- Eligibility for retirement is age 55 with 10 years of service.

Hypothetical employee characteristics:
- age at hire = 45
- normal retirement age = 65
- total service = 20 years
- service to earliest eligibility for retirement = 10 years

Accrual Method	Age 50, still working	Age 55, still working	Age 65, retiring
Accrual at retirement	0%	0%	80%
Accrual at eligibility for retirement	0	80	80
Ratable accrual from date of hire to age 65 (accrued benefit = current service/20 × 80%)	20	40	80
Ratable accrual from date of hire to earliest eligibility for retirement (accrued benefit = current service/10 × 80%)	40	80	80
Ratable accrual over 25 years (accrued benefit = current service/25 × 80%)	16	32	64

Accrued Benefit at Sample Ages (employer's share of total cost)

applied to each of the sample groups in this study. The term "accrued benefit liabilities" refers to the present value of future benefits accrued to date under the stated accrual method. These liabilities are based on the closed group projections developed in chapters I through III. Discussions among policymakers regarding the desirability of making benefits portable imply some form of accrual method such as those illustrated here.

Cessation of Employer Operations

If an employer were to cease operations, the present value of future benefits for current employees could change immediately. In the case

TABLE IV.2
Comparison of Accrued Benefit Liabilities under Alternative Accrual Methods (millions)

Accrual Method	Accrued Benefit Liabilities		
	Group A (stable)	Group F (older)	Group H (new)
Accrual at retirement			
PVFB[a]: retirees	$23.8	$43.0	$ 0.3
vested[b] employees	0.0	0.0	0.0
nonvested[b] employees	0.0	0.0	0.0
total	23.8	43.0	0.3
Accrual at eligibility for retirement			
PVFB[a]: retirees	23.8	43.0	0.3
vested[b] employees	8.9	20.0	0.6
nonvested[b] employees	0.0	0.0	0.0
total	32.7	63.0	0.9
Ratable accrual from date of hire to age 65			
PVFB[a]: retirees	23.8	43.0	0.3
vested[b] employees	6.8	16.2	0.4
nonvested[b] employees	16.6	14.7	21.2
total	47.2	73.9	21.9
Ratable accrual from date of hire to earliest eligibility for retirement			
PVFB[a]: retirees	23.8	43.0	0.3
vested[b] employees	8.9	20.0	0.6
nonvested[b] employees	23.6	20.8	30.9
total	56.3	83.8	31.8

[a]Present value of future benefits.
[b]The terms "vested" and "nonvested," as used here, refer to employees that are currently eligible to retire with benefits and those that are not currently eligible, respectively.

of a cessation of operations, if all employees eligible to retire begin to receive medical benefits immediately, actual benefit payments for those individuals will often be significantly higher than those projected under assumptions of a continuation of operations. For other employees, there will be no future benefit payments unless there are vesting provisions that guarantee a nonforfeitable right to benefits currently accrued and to be paid at some future date.

TABLE IV.3
Comparison of Accrued Benefit Liabilities for Current Employees: Continuation of Operations vs. Cessation (millions)

	PVFB[a] for Vested Employees[b]			Accrued PVFB[a] for Nonvested Employees[c]		
	Group A (stable)	Group F (older)	Group H (new)	Group A (stable)	Group F (older)	Group H (new)
Continuation of employer operations						
under age 65	$ 1.5	$ 4.0	$ 0.1	$ 5.3	$ 5.6	$ 5.4
age 65 and over	7.4	16.0	0.5	18.3	15.2	25.5
total	8.9	20.0	0.6	23.6	20.8	30.9
Cessation of employer operations						
under age 65	5.5	11.5	0.5	37.0	43.2	34.3
age 65 and over	7.4	16.0	0.5	32.2	37.1	31.4
total	12.9	27.5	1.0	69.2	80.3	65.7
Percent increase in PVFB[a] for current employees due to cessation						
under age 65	267%	188%	400%	598%	671%	535%
age 65 and over	0	0	0	76	144	23
total	45	38	67	193	286	113

[a]Present value of future benefits.
[b]Vested employees are those eligible to retire immediately with benefits.
[c]Accrued ratably from date of hire to earliest eligibility for retirement. Accrued benefits for nonvested employees are lost upon cessation unless special vesting is granted.

Table IV.3 compares the present value of future benefits for current employees under a cessation-of-employer-operations scenario with those based on an assumed continuation of operations. Values are shown for currently vested employees (i.e., those eligible to retire with benefits) and for accrued benefits of nonvested employees, using ratable accrual to earliest eligibility for retirement. These accrued benefits for nonvested employees would not represent a benefit liability upon cessation of operations unless vesting were granted. For these groups, benefit liabilities for employees eligible to retire (i.e., those vested) are increased from 38 to 67 percent due to the cessation of operations.

TABLE IV.4
Comparison of Accrued Benefit Liabilities for Current Employees: Continuation of Operations vs. Cessation Early Retirement Rates = Twice Original Rates
(millions)

	PVFB[a] for Vested Employees[b]			Accrued PVFB[a] for Nonvested Employees[c]		
	Group A (stable)	Group F (older)	Group H (new)	Group A (stable)	Group F (older)	Group H (new)
Continuation of employer operations						
under age 65	$ 2.2	$ 5.7	$ 0.2	$ 7.9	$ 8.3	$ 8.2
age 65 and over	7.4	16.0	0.5	18.3	15.2	25.5
total	9.6	21.7	0.7	26.2	23.5	33.7
Cessation of employer operations						
under age 65	5.5	11.5	0.5	37.0	43.2	34.3
age 65 and over	7.4	16.0	0.5	32.2	37.1	31.4
total	12.9	27.5	1.0	69.2	80.3	65.7
Percent increase in PVFB[a] for current employees due to cessation						
under age 65	150%	102%	150%	368%	420%	318%
age 65 and over	0	0	0	76	144	23
total	34	27	43	164	242	95

[a]Present value of future benefits.
[b]Vested employees are those eligible to retire immediately with benefits.
[c]Accrued ratably from date of hire to earliest eligibility for retirement. Accrued benefits for nonvested employees are lost upon cessation unless special vesting is granted.

The accrued benefits for those not eligible to retire (i.e., nonvested employees) are increased from 113 to 286 percent, assuming that such benefits would become payable at the earliest retirement age. If these benefits were not vested and, therefore, not payable under any conditions, there would be no remaining liability for these amounts in the event of cessation.

If early retirement rates are doubled, the impact of cessation is decreased because more retirements have already been anticipated. Table IV.4 presents the same values as table IV.3, but under the assumption that early retirement rates at ages 55 to 64 are doubled for all groups. For groups with these higher early retirement rates, cessation of operations would still increase benefit liabilities for vested employees by from 27 to 43 percent, and those for accrued benefits of nonvested employees by from 95 to 242 percent.

Part Two
Funding Scenarios (Open Group)

V. Methods for Funding and Expensing of Retiree Medical Benefits

This chapter discusses the principles of advance funding and expensing of postretirement medical benefits. Several common pension funding methods are described, as are three modified funding methods that are applied to retiree medical benefits in this study.

Most employers currently pay for retiree medical benefits on a pay-as-you-go basis. The benefits are recognized as an expense in the year they are paid, and no special fund is set up in advance for their payment. While not common in practice, it is possible to apply various methods for advance funding of these benefits and/or for expensing them during the working lives of the affected employees.

Advance funding involves making contributions to a special fund designated for future payment of benefits. The fund builds up over time through direct contributions and investment earnings. Each year the benefit amounts paid are withdrawn from the fund.

The concept of expensing for benefits, on the other hand, is an accounting principle. Each year, the cost of future benefits that is attributable to current operations is charged as an expense on the income statement. If benefits are expensed in this manner, the cumulative value of such annual expense costs in excess of actual contributions to date is recognized as a liability on the corporate balance sheet.

While these two functions serve different purposes, there are issues common to both. Two common requirements are:

(1) *Method of Projecting Future Benefit Costs*—The estimation of future benefit costs involves a projection of the covered population, assumptions regarding current per capita plan costs and their future rate of growth, and choosing an appropriate discount rate.

(2) *Method of Allocating the Projected Future Benefit Costs to Years of Active Employment*—A number of methods have been developed to allocate the costs of a pension plan; these can also be applied to retiree medical benefits. Several of these methods are described below.

Retiree Medical Funding Methods (Pension Techniques)

For a pension plan that meets qualifications for tax deductibility, as specified by ERISA, annual funding contributions are fully tax-deductible within the limits established by the IRS. These limits are expressed in terms of specific funding methods. Three of the more widely used methods are the Entry Age Normal method, the Projected Unit Credit method, and the Aggregate method. All three are likely candidates for direct application as retiree medical funding methods. Each determines the normal cost (the cost that is assigned to a given plan year) in a unique way.

Entry Age Normal

The Entry Age Normal funding method values the ultimate projected benefit for each individual. This benefit is the present value of the plan cost for each year that the individual is projected to receive benefits. The value of this total projected benefit is then allocated to each year of that individual's employment as a level annual cost. The total normal cost for the plan in a given year is the sum of the allocated costs for each individual in the plan during that year.

The level annual cost for each employee can be determined as a level dollar amount each year, or as a level percentage of salary (changing each year in proportion to the change in salary). The Entry Age Normal method used in this study uses the level-percentage-of-salary approach.

Projected Unit Credit

Under the Projected Unit Credit funding method, the projected benefit for each individual is treated as if it is earned ratably over that individual's period of employment, from the date of hire to the date of retirement. The total normal cost for the plan in a given year, then, is the sum of the costs of the benefits "earned" by each individual in that year.

Aggregate

The Aggregate funding method values the total projected benefits for all individuals, measured from the current year of service. The cost for these total projected benefits is then spread over the future working lives of all individuals as a level percentage of salary. The normal cost for the plan is then derived by applying this level percentage to the current year's aggregate salary.

Pattern of Normal Costs

The Entry Age Normal and Projected Unit Credit methods are quite similar; when applied to the model groups in this study, the resulting patterns show no material differences. Each spreads the cost of the projected benefit for a given individual over his or her period of employment.

Under the Entry Age Normal method, an equal cost is allocated to each year of employment, producing a pattern of costs that are level, as a percentage of salary, for a given individual. Under the Projected Unit Credit method, the cost of an equal portion of the benefit is allocated to each year of employment. This cost is the present value of that portion of the benefit payable at retirement. Therefore, the cost increases each year as the employee grows closer to his or her retirement age.

Either of these methods could produce higher normal costs; for a given group, the relative pattern of costs will depend on the assumed rate of growth in salary, the discount rate, and probabilities of termination prior to retirement. In most cases, however, the overall pattern of normal costs is similar under these two methods. The normal costs produced by the Aggregate method will always be higher initially than those produced by the Entry Age Normal or Projected Unit Credit methods. As a percentage of total salary, the normal costs under the Aggregate method will decline gradually.

Funding of Initial Liability

The Aggregate method differs considerably from the other two methods with respect to the way it operates in an initial funding situation—i.e., when funding is first adopted for a plan that has been in existence for some time.

The Aggregate method deals with this situation indirectly; normal costs are higher in the initial funding years than they would have been if funding had been in place from the plan's inception. These excess costs are, in effect, spread gradually over the working lives of all employees currently in the plan. If funding is initiated when most employees are approaching retirement, their average future working life is short, so the required contribution is quite high.

Under the Entry Age Normal and Projected Unit Credit methods, however, the normal cost at the time of initial funding is the same as it would have been if funding had occurred in the past. The amount that would have been built up through past funding, called the initial unfunded liability, is amortized over a specified period of time, such as 30 years.

The total annual contribution during the period of amortization, then, is equal to the normal cost plus the amortization payment.[1]

---

[1]The actual annual contribution applicable under any of the funding methods described here is, in practice, also affected by other factors. These include gains and losses that arise when actual demographic or economic experience differs from the experience estimates (actuarial assumptions), changes in unfunded liabilities due to

After the amortization period is over, the fund would be at the same level as it would have been if funding had been in place from the inception of the plan, and the contribution would then be equal to the normal cost.

In pension funding, an employer has some flexibility in choosing the amortization period for the initial unfunded liability (as well as any future gains or losses) under the Entry Age Normal or Projected Unit Credit methods.

In the funding scenarios presented at the end of this study, both a minimum and maximum amortization period are illustrated. The following terminology has been adopted for these approaches:

(1) "Maximum deductible" refers to the minimum amortization period allowed for tax-deductibility of pension contributions, which is 10 years.

(2) "Minimum ERISA" refers to the maximum amortization period prescribed by ERISA; generally, this is 30 years for the unfunded liability and 15 years for gains and losses.

Modified Advance Funding Methods for RetireeMedical Benefits

The importance of economic assumptions in projections of retiree medical benefits has led to discussions of alternative funding methods that deal explicitly with the relationship between the assumed trend and the discount rate. The funding scenarios presented in this study demonstrate the application of three such approaches to the model groups.

Two of these approaches (Unprojected Unit Credit and Unit Credit with No Trend or Discount Rate) have been included because they reflect methods proposed for application to retiree medical benefits in other studies. The third method (Projected Unit Credit with Trend Equal to Per Capita GNP Growth Rate) is presented here as a third alternative.

These three methods are variations of the Projected Unit Credit method; in each, future benefits are projected using assumptions other than best estimates. They will be referred to here as "modified advance funding methods," while the original methods described above will be referred to as "full funding methods."

---

changes in actuarial assumptions, and the minimum and maximum funding limitations of the Internal Revenue Code. These factors are illustrated in the funding scenarios presented in the appendices to this study.

Briefly, the three modified advance funding methods considered are as follows.

Unprojected Unit Credit

The Unprojected Unit Credit method operates in the same way as the Projected Unit Credit method, except that future benefits are projected under the assumption that per capita plan costs will remain at their current level (i.e., that the medical trend in all future years will be 0 percent). As actual per capita plan costs increase from year to year, the increase is recognized in the current year's normal cost. The effect of the increase in each year is treated as an actuarial loss and spread over future years. The method is included here because Internal Revenue Code section 419A requires its use for voluntary employee beneficiary associations (VEBAs).

Unit Credit with No Trend or Discount Rate

This unit credit method also operates in the same way as the Projected Unit Credit method, except that future benefits are projected using both a trend assumption of 0 percent and a discount rate of 0 percent. This approach would be similar to using trend and discount rates that are equal, since, in the calculation of present values, an equal trend and discount rate will offset each other.

Projected Unit Credit with Trend Equal to Per Capita GNP Growth Rate

In addition to these two methods, a third variation of the Projected Unit Credit method is also considered in this study: Projected Unit Credit with the trend limited to the assumed rate of growth in per capita GNP. Based on the relationships between economic assumptions developed in chapter I, this would mean that trend is limited to the discount rate less 2 percent. Since a 7 percent discount rate is used in this study, this is equivalent to a 5 percent cap on the trend.

Expensing for Retiree Medical Benefits

Statement of Financial Accounting Standards Number 87 (SFAS 87), "Employers' Accounting for Pensions," prescribes the methodology that must be used for expensing pension benefits for fiscal years beginning on or after December 15, 1986. SFAS 87 prescribes a Projected Unit Credit approach with amortization of any net unfunded liability and future gains and losses over the average expected working lives of employees expected to receive benefits.

This method, or others, could be applied to the expensing of retiree medical benefits. In the funding scenarios presented in chapters VI through VIII, SFAS 87 standards have been applied to derive the annual expenses applicable to each scenario; annual expenses under each funding scenario are summarized in appendix B. These expense levels are affected by the level of funding that occurs under the given scenario, in that the interest charge on liabilities is offset by the expected return on actual fund assets.

VI. Funding Scenarios: General Approach

This chapter discusses the approach taken in this study to analyze funding patterns, using the model groups. The open group projection methodology is described and the rationale for selection of economic assumptions is discussed.

The funding patterns that occur when a range of alternative funding methods is applied to the retiree medical benefits of each of the model groups are analyzed. These results are presented as a series of funding scenarios. Each funding scenario involves the application of a given funding method to one of the model groups over a 50-year period under one of several economic scenarios. These economic scenarios represent levels of actual medical care trends that might occur throughout the 50-year period.

Detailed results of the funding scenarios are summarized in appendices B, C, and D. Chapters VII and VIII discuss some of the significant patterns that emerge in the scenarios.

Open Group Assumptions

The funding scenarios are based on 50-year open group projections of each of the model groups; in other words, new entrants in future years are taken into account. Actual fund buildup is then tracked over the 50-year period. Group F (older, declining group) is projected under two separate assumptions as to the rate of decline—a 2 percent annual rate of decline and a 7 percent rate. Results for Group F are presented under both of these projection assumptions. Table VI.1 summarizes the projected employee and retiree populations of each group for selected years under these open group projections.

Group F was projected at a 7 percent rate of decline to demonstrate the funding patterns that develop in a rapidly declining group; the ratio of retirees to active workers under that projection exceeds two to one by year 30.

Based on the projected populations of employees and retirees over the 50-year period, annual funding contributions are calculated for each group under several different funding methods. In these funding scenarios, only those employees that actually meet the eligibility requirements (i.e., age 55 with 10 years of service) are entitled to receive

TABLE VI.1
Open Group Projection Results: Population Counts for Selected Years (thousands)

	Group A (Stable)			Group F (Older, Declining)						Group H (New)		
				2% rate of decline			7% rate of decline					
			Retirees per			Retirees per			Retirees per			Retirees per
Year	Employees	Retirees	employee	Employees	Retirees	employee	Employees	Retirees	employee	Employees	Retirees	employee
0	10.0	1.6	0.2	10.0	3.0	0.3	10.0	3.0	0.3	10.0	—	—
10	12.2	2.5	0.2	8.2	4.0	0.5	4.8	4.0	0.8	12.2	1.3	0.1
20	14.9	3.4	0.2	6.7	4.0	0.6	2.3	3.7	1.6	14.9	3.6	0.2
30	18.1	4.8	0.3	5.5	3.3	0.6	1.1	2.6	2.4	18.1	6.0	0.3
40	22.1	6.4	0.3	4.5	2.5	0.6	0.5	1.4	2.8	22.1	8.5	0.4
50	26.9	7.9	0.3	3.6	2.0	0.6	0.3	0.7	2.3	26.9	10.4	0.4

40

benefits; no vesting is granted to employees that leave prior to retirement.

Economic Scenarios

As discussed in chapter I, the present value of future retiree medical benefits depends on the relationship between the assumed annual trend and the discount rate. Because funding contributions are based on present value calculations, the contributions and fund buildup are affected by these assumptions. In the funding scenarios, the level of benefits paid out each year also depends on the annual trend assumption.

The long-range trend assumptions were selected based on assumed long-term relationships between certain key economic factors. These relationships, which were discussed in chapter I, are as follows:

discount rate = 7 percent
general rate of inflation = discount rate − 3.5 percent = 3.5 percent
rate of growth in per capita GNP = general rate of inflation
   + 1.5 percent = 5 percent

Given these assumptions, then, alternative trend scenarios were chosen (designated as low, medium, and high). In each case, the trend rate started at 10 percent in year one and gradually declined to 5 percent (the rate of growth in per capita GNP). The initial rate of 10 percent reflects a 6.5-point spread between medical care inflation and overall inflation; this is the general order of magnitude of the spread that has developed between these two values in recent years.

The trend values for future years were selected by considering a likely range of ultimate levels of the medical care component of total GNP. They were derived by assuming that medical care currently constitutes 11 percent of GNP and that it will grow to an ultimate level of GNP as follows:

low scenario: 17 percent
medium scenario: 22 percent
high scenario: 29 percent

This is the ultimate level of the medical care component of GNP under each scenario by the time the trend levels off at 5 percent.

Table VI.2 summarizes the economic assumptions for each scenario. These scenarios are not intended to accurately forecast economic patterns or to predict the magnitude of the medical care component of the GNP. Rather, they are designed to provide a reasonable range

TABLE VI.2
Summary of Economic Assumptions

	Low Scenario	Medium Scenario	High Scenario
Rate of general inflation	3.5%	3.5%	3.5%
Rate of growth in per capita GNP[a]	5.0	5.0	5.0
Discount rate	7.0	7.0	7.0
Medical trend		years	
10%	1–3	1–5	1–7
9	4–6	6–10	8–14
8	7–9	11–15	15–21
7	10–12	16–20	22–28
6	13–15	21–25	29–35
5	16–50	26–50	36–50
Medical care as percentage of GNP			
current	11%	11%	11%
ultimate	17	22	29

[a]Gross National Product.

of results over a 50-year projection period. The test for reasonableness here, as discussed in chapter I, is that medical care costs are not likely to rise to more than about 30 percent of GNP.

Clearly, the basic relationships between the economic factors assumed are subject to variation. Their absolute levels could also vary significantly from those assumed. However, since it is the relationship between the trend and discount rate that affects the pattern of funding contributions, varying their absolute values while keeping the same spread would not produce dramatic changes in the general patterns produced by these assumptions.

Taxes

All funding scenarios presented in this study assume no tax impact. Current rules would not provide employer deductions for contributions of the magnitude shown, nor would the funds accumulated automatically qualify for tax-free accumulation. The subject of the tax effect is beyond the scope of this study.

VII. Comparison of Funding Patterns

This chapter discusses the funding patterns that develop when various funding methods are applied to the model groups. The pattern of annual contributions and rate of fund buildup under each method are compared, and comparisons of advance funding and pay-as-you-go funding are made by group.

Appendix B includes summaries of the funding values described here. The six funding methods used in these scenarios are those discussed in chapter V.

Annual Contributions

The annual contribution made to the fund each year is as follows:

annual contribution = normal cost
                + amortization payment (if applicable)[1]

Under the funding rules that have been applied in these scenarios (i.e., those that currently apply to tax-qualified pension plans), this contribution is subject to certain limitations designed to prevent overfunding. This "full funding limitation" does not allow an employer to make a contribution if the current fund already exceeds current benefit obligations (as defined for that funding method).

In each of the three trend scenarios considered (low, medium, and high), the assumed trend is 10 percent in year one and declines over time. In each year, benefit projections are made by assuming that the current trend remains constant in all future years. For example, in the first year all funding calculations are based on the assumption that trend will be 10 percent in future years.

Table VII.1 compares annual funding contributions for Group A under the three full funding methods considered, based on the medium trend scenario. It also illustrates some general patterns common to each of the model groups and to each trend scenario, as follows.

(1) Contributions are slightly higher under the Entry Age Normal method than under the Projected Unit Credit method; however, the two methods follow a similar pattern.

---

[1]Amortization payment does not apply to the Aggregate funding method.

(2) Aggregate method contributions most closely resemble those of the Entry Age Normal—Minimum basis. While slightly higher initially, contributions under the Aggregate method fall slightly below the Entry Age Normal contributions in later years.

(3) After the first 10 years, there is little variation in the contributions under any of these methods.

The annual contributions that develop under the three modified advance funding methods are summarized in table VII.2. Some general patterns illustrated in table VII.2 also apply to the other model groups and to other trend scenarios, as follows.

(1) The Unprojected Unit Credit method has the lowest contributions initially; after 30 to 40 years, however, contributions under this method are slightly higher than under the other methods.

(2) The contributions under all three methods are fairly close after 30 years and are quite similar to those under the Projected Unit Credit method. (The funds that accumulate under these methods vary significantly, however, as discussed below.)

Comparison with Pay-As-You-Go Funding

Pay-as-you-go funding refers to the payment of benefit costs as they are incurred. Annual payments are equal to the current year's benefit payments, and no fund is accumulated.

TABLE VII.1
Comparison of Annual Contributions: Full Funding Methods, Group A (Stable), Medium Trend Scenario (millions)

Year	Entry Age Normal Maximum	Entry Age Normal Minimum	Projected Unit Credit Maximum	Projected Unit Credit Minimum	Aggregate
0	$ 20	$ 14	$ 16	$ 11	$ 15
5	27	21	21	16	20
10	18	21	16	18	19
15	20	20	19	19	19
20	24	24	23	23	22
25	28	28	27	27	25
30	32	32	30	30	27
35	46	46	42	42	42
40	66	66	60	60	61
45	93	93	84	84	88
50	131	131	119	119	126

Note: Minimum contributions exceed maximum contributions in some years due to effects of full funding limitations.

TABLE VII.2
Comparison of Annual Contributions: Modified Advance Funding Methods, Group A (Stable), Medium Trend Scenario (millions)

Year	Unprojected Unit Credit Maximum	Unprojected Unit Credit Minimum	No Trend or Discount Rate Maximum	No Trend or Discount Rate Minimum	Trend Equal to Per Capita GNP[a] Growth Rate Maximum	Trend Equal to Per Capita GNP[a] Growth Rate Minimum
0	$ 3	$ 2	$ 9	$ 6	$ 6	$ 4
5	5	4	12	9	9	7
10	6	6	14	14	11	11
15	9	10	17	21	14	16
20	14	15	23	29	20	24
25	21	22	28	33	27	31
30	31	31	30	30	32	36
35	44	44	43	43	42	42
40	62	62	60	60	60	60
45	87	87	85	85	84	84
50	122	122	120	120	119	119

[a]Gross National Product.
Note: Minimum contributions exceed maximum contributions in some years due to effects of full funding limitations.

Charts VII.1a through VII.1d compare annual pay-as-you-go costs with the annual contributions under the Projected Unit Credit—Minimum method for each group under the medium trend scenario. The following patterns can be observed from these charts.

(1) For groups A and H, which are growing at an annual rate of 2 percent, pay-as-you-go payments approach the level of the advance funding contributions but do not exceed them within the 50-year period.

(2) For Group F, which is projected at two annual rates of decline, pay-as-you-go payments begin to exceed advance funding payments after 15 to 20 years; thereafter, pay-as-you-go payments grow rapidly in relation to advance funding contributions.

At the end of 50 years, funds of $2.5 billion and $3.4 billion have accumulated under the advance funding approach for groups A and H, respectively; no fund has accumulated under the pay-as-you-go approach. The liabilities for retirees and vested employees combined are $1.9 billion for Group A and $2.6 billion for Group H. For Group F, a fund of $0.1 to $0.4 billion has accumulated after 50 years under the advance funding approach.

CHART VII.1a
Comparison of Pay-As-You-Go and Full Funding Methods
Group A (Stable—2% Growth): Medium Trend Scenario

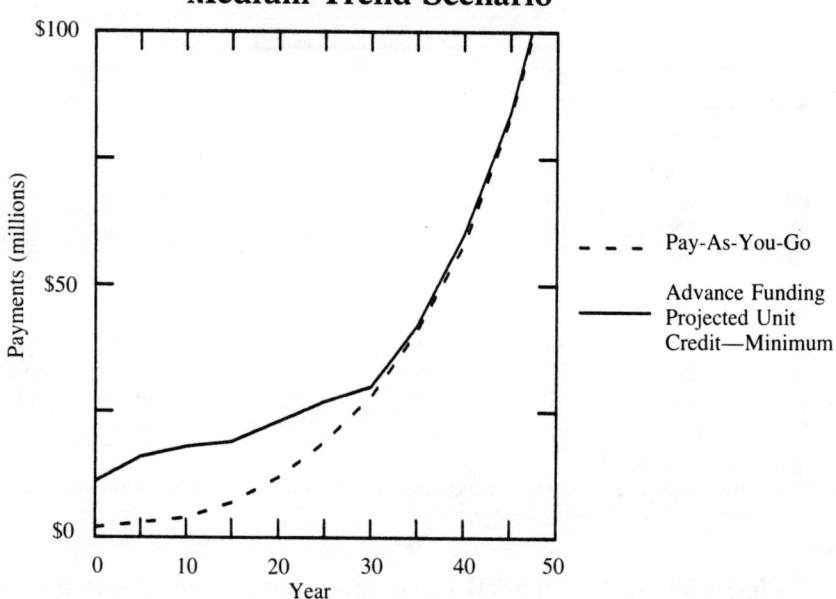

[Chart showing Payments (millions) from $0 to $100 over Years 0 to 50, comparing Pay-As-You-Go (dashed line) and Advance Funding Projected Unit Credit—Minimum (solid line)]

If pay-as-you-go funding is used until year 50, for all groups the cost to begin funding in year 50 would be about three times the funding cost that would result in that year if funding was started in the first year of the projection.

Fund Accumulation

The fund that accumulates under an advance funding method is equal to the contributions made, plus investment earnings on the fund, less benefits paid out. Under a funding method that has higher contributions in the earlier years, the fund builds more rapidly; as a result, annual investment earnings are higher than under a method that funds more slowly. Over time, the annual contributions under both types of methods will tend to grow closer as the investment earnings play an increasing role in the fund accumulation of the more rapid method.

Table VII.3 and chart VII.2 compare the fund buildup that occurs for Group A under the three full funding methods. They illustrate the

CHART VII.1b
Comparison of Pay-As-You-Go and Full Funding Methods Group F (Older—2% Decline): Medium Trend Scenario

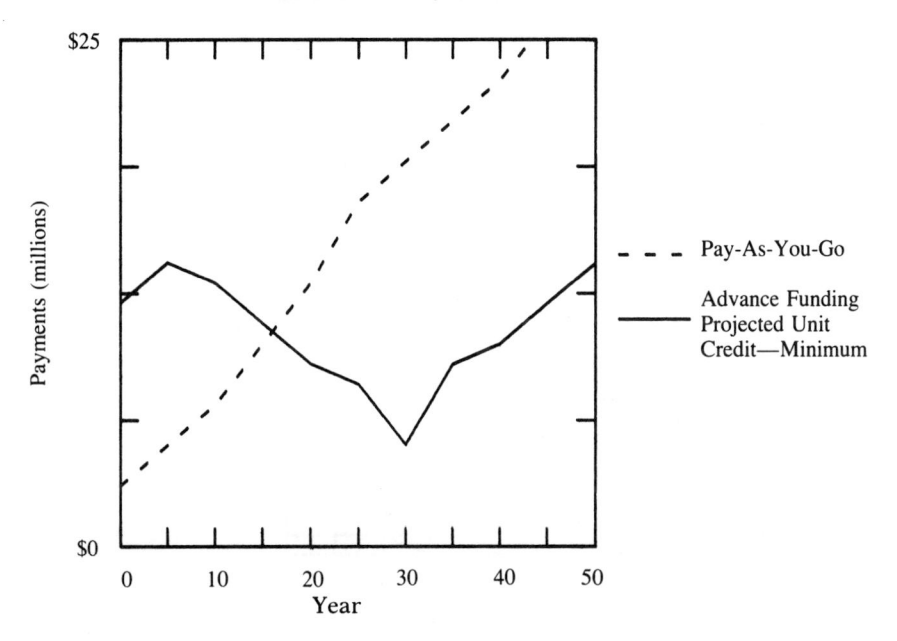

following patterns, which apply generally to each of the model groups and each trend scenario.

(1) Initially, fund accumulation is more rapid under the Entry Age Normal method than under either the Projected Unit Credit or Aggregate methods.

(2) In general, for a stable or growing group, the fund buildup under all of these methods is similar after the first 10 years or so.

The fund accumulation that occurs under the modified advance funding methods for Group A is illustrated in table VII.4. The following patterns are evident from this comparison and also apply to the other model groups and other trend scenarios.

(1) The fund that accumulates under the Unprojected Unit Credit method is substantially lower than that under any of the other methods considered.

CHART VII.1c
Comparison of Pay-As-You-Go and Full Funding Methods Group F (Older—7% Decline): Medium Trend Scenario

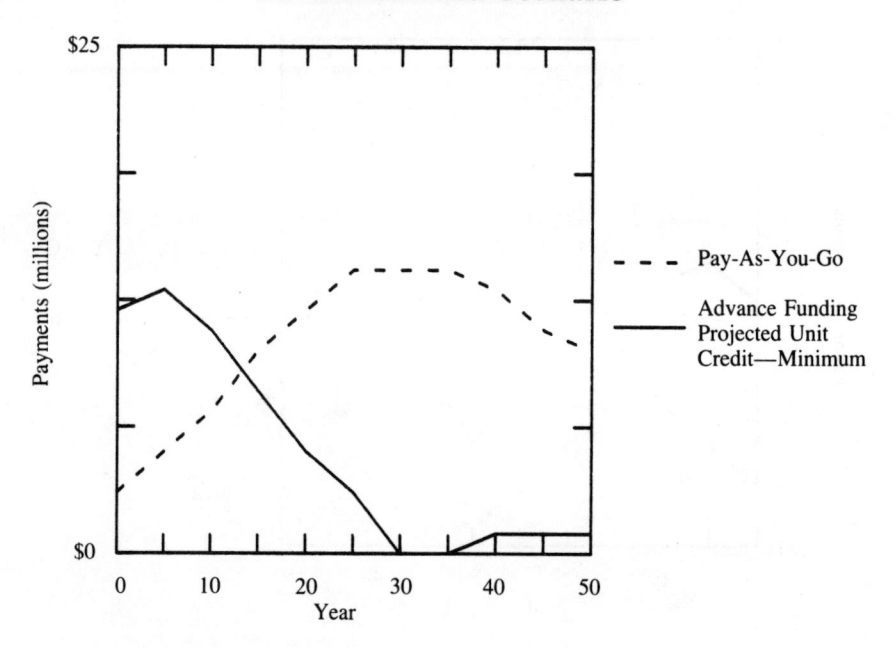

- - - Pay-As-You-Go

—— Advance Funding Projected Unit Credit—Minimum

(2) The Unit Credit Method with No Trend or Discount Rate results in a higher fund than either of the other modified advance funding methods. After year 20, the fund under this method is also higher than that under any of the full funding methods. This is because in the medium trend scenario the annual trend drops below the discount rate in year 21. Therefore, the benefit values produced by the full funding methods at that point will be lower than those based on an assumption that the trend and discount rate are equal (which is, in effect, what this alternative unit credit method assumes).

(3) After year 25, when the annual trend drops to 5 percent, the fund that accumulates under the Projected Unit Credit Method with Trend Equal to per Capita GNP Growth Rate is essentially the same as that under the Projected Unit Credit method. As long as the trend stays at or below 5 percent, these methods will be identical (except for any differences in amortization payments arising from prior periods).

Costs Per Employee

Table VII.5 summarizes the first-year costs for two funding methods in terms of a cost per employee (all groups are assumed to have 10,000

CHART VII.1d
Comparison of Pay-As-You-Go and Full Funding Methods
Group H (New—2% Growth): Medium Trend Scenario

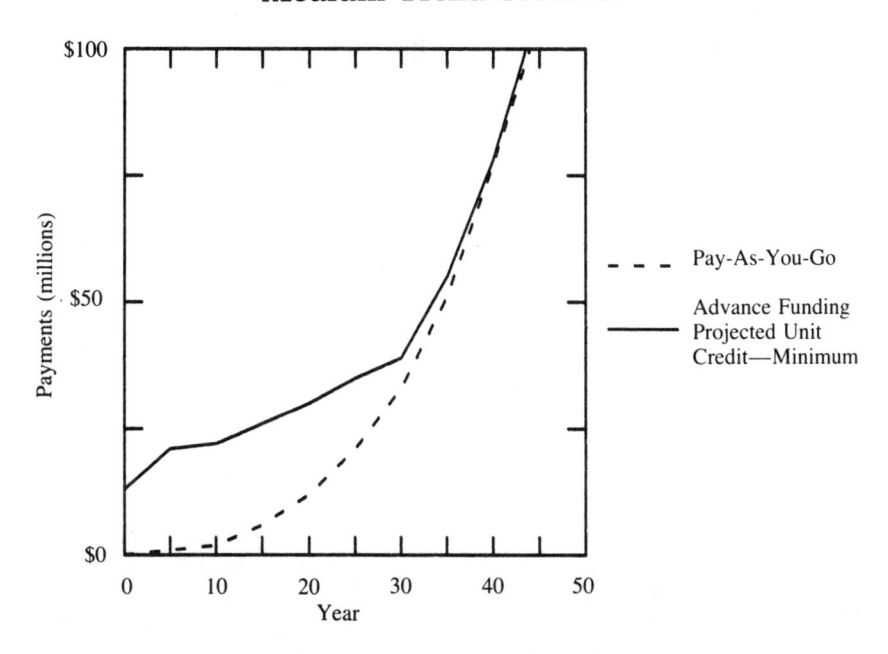

employees in the first year). The pay-as-you-go cost for that year is also shown on the same basis. For groups with higher per capita plan costs than those used in this study, the first-year funding costs would be proportionately higher than those shown in tables VII.6a through VII.6d, which illustrate the pattern of costs per employee over the 50-year projection period for the three groups: Group A (stable), Group F (older, with 2 percent and 7 percent rates of decline), and Group H (new). Pay-as-you-go and Projected Unit Credit—Minimum approaches are included; the cost per employee for each is shown for selected years. Note in table VII.6c the typical cost pattern for a group that is in a period of decline: as the ratio of retirees to employees grows, the pay-as-you-go cost per employee grows rapidly. On the other hand, advance funding costs per employee tend to remain more stable.

The fund that accumulates under the advance funding methods is available to pay future benefits in the case of a cessation of the plan

TABLE VII.3
Comparison of Fund Accumulation: Full Funding Methods, Group A (Stable), Medium Trend Scenario (millions)

Year	Entry Age Normal Maximum	Entry Age Normal Mimimum	Projected Unit Credit Maximum	Projected Unit Credit Minimum	Aggregate
0	$ 0	$ 0	$ 0	$ 0	$ 0
5	115	80	88	62	84
10	235	192	188	154	193
15	322	322	274	274	318
20	426	426	375	375	426
25	544	544	492	492	544
30	668	668	617	617	667
35	944	943	878	878	918
40	1,334	1,331	1,243	1,243	1,273
45	1,885	1,879	1,753	1,753	1,775
50	2,658	2,649	2,470	2,470	2,482

or of employer operations. Under the pay-as-you-go approach, however, there is no such fund.

Charts VII.3a through VII.3d illustrate these annual funding costs as a percentage of payroll, based on assumed average salaries in the first year of $15,000 or $30,000; per capita salaries are assumed to increase 5 percent per year. Note the following in reviewing these charts.

(1) The advance funding method illustrated is Projected Unit Credit—Minimum; however, any of the full funding methods would produce generally similar patterns.

(2) Because benefit costs are not dependent on salary, the percentage of payroll values vary in proportion to average salaries. For example, if the initial average salary is $30,000, costs as a percentage of payroll are exactly one-half as great as they are if the initial average salary is $15,000.

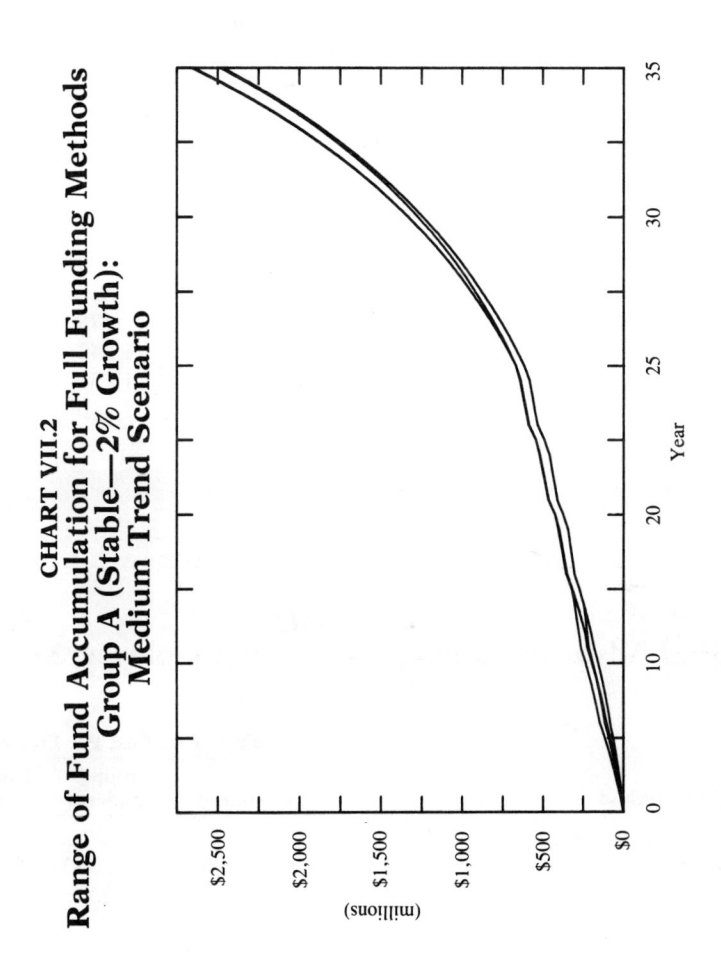

CHART VII.2
Range of Fund Accumulation for Full Funding Methods Group A (Stable—2% Growth): Medium Trend Scenario

TABLE VII.4
Comparison of Fund Accumulation: Modified Advance Funding Methods, Group A (Stable), Medium Trend Scenario (millions)

Year	Unprojected Unit Credit Maximum	Unprojected Unit Credit Minimum	No Trend or Discount Rate Maximum	No Trend or Discount Rate Minimum	Trend Equal to Per Capita GNP[a] Growth Rate Maximum	Trend Equal to Per Capita GNP[a] Growth Rate Minimum
0	$ 0	$ 0	$ 0	$ 0	$ 0	$ 0
5	8	2	44	28	29	17
10	27	11	118	83	78	52
15	49	30	222	182	151	117
20	81	60	375	342	256	224
25	128	104	577	572	409	385
30	196	167	832	833	615	604
35	294	251	1,182	1,183	878	879
40	433	372	1,670	1,671	1,243	1,243
45	632	546	2,355	2,356	1,753	1,753
50	914	794	3,317	3,319	2,470	2,470

[a]Gross National Product.

TABLE VII.5
Initial Advance Funding Costs Per Employee, Medium Trend Scenario

Funding Method	First-Year Cost Per Employee Group A (stable)	Group F (older)	Group H (new)
Projected Unit Credit			
maximum	$1,600	$1,900	$1,600
minimum	1,100	1,200	1,300
Unit Credit with Trend Equal to Per Capita GNP[a] Growth Rate			
maximum	600	900	400
minimum	400	600	400
Pay-as-you-go	200	300	—

[a]Gross National Product.

TABLE VII.6a
Comparison of Funding Costs Per Employee by Year Group A (Stable—2% Growth), Medium Trend Scenario Projected Unit Credit—Minimum

				Cost Per Employee	
Year	Number of Employees	Number of Retirees	Retirees Per Employee	Pay-as-you-go	Advance funding
0	10,000	1,600	0.2	$ 200	$1,100
10	12,200	2,500	0.2	328	1,475
20	14,900	3,400	0.2	805	1,544
30	18,100	4,800	0.3	1,547	1,657
40	22,100	6,400	0.3	2,624	2,715
50	26,900	7,900	0.3	4,349	4,424
				Fund in Year 50 (millions)	
				$ 0	$2,470

TABLE VII.6b
Comparison of Funding Costs Per Employee by Year Group F (Older—2% Decline), Medium Trend Scenario Projected Unit Credit—Minimum

				Cost Per Employee	
Year	Number of Employees	Number of Retirees	Retirees Per Employee	Pay-as-you-go	Advance funding
0	10,000	3,000	0.3	$ 300	$1,200
10	8,200	4,000	0.5	854	1,585
20	6,700	4,000	0.6	1,940	1,343
30	5,500	3,300	0.6	3,455	909
40	4,500	2,500	0.6	5,111	2,222
50	3,600	2,000	0.6	8,333	3,889
				Fund in Year 50 (millions)	
				$ 0	$ 417

TABLE VII.6c
Comparison of Funding Costs Per Employee by Year
Group F (Older—7% Decline), Medium Trend Scenario
Projected Unit Credit—Minimum

				Cost Per Employee	
Year	Number of Employees	Number of Retirees	Retirees Per Employee	Pay-as-you-go	Advance funding
0	10,000	3,000	0.3	$ 300	$1,200
10	5,100	4,000	0.8	1,373	2,157
20	2,600	3,700	1.4	4,615	1,923
30	1,300	2,600	2.0	10,769	0
40	700	1,400	2.0	18,571	1,429
50	300	700	2.3	33,333	3,333
				Fund in Year 50 (millions)	
				$ 0	$ 97

TABLE VII.6d
Comparison of Funding Costs Per Employee by Year
Group H (New—2% Growth), Medium Trend Scenario
Projected Unit Credit—Minimum

				Cost Per Employee	
Year	Number of Employees	Number of Retirees	Retirees Per Employee	Pay-as-you-go	Advance funding
0	10,000	0	0.0	$ 0	$1,300
10	12,200	1,300	0.1	164	1,803
20	14,900	3,600	0.2	805	2,013
30	18,100	6,000	0.3	1,823	2,155
40	22,100	8,500	0.4	3,484	3,529
50	26,900	10,400	0.4	5,576	5,725
				Fund in Year 50 (millions)	
				$ 0	$3,412

CHART VII.3a
Funding Costs As Percentage of Payroll by Year Group A (Stable—2% Growth): Medium Trend Scenario

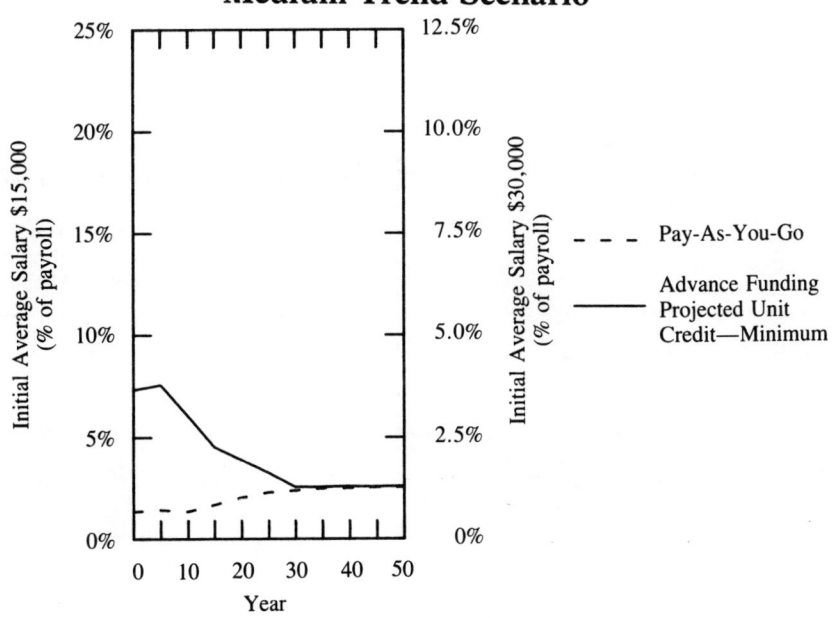

- - - Pay-As-You-Go

——— Advance Funding Projected Unit Credit—Minimum

CHART VII.3b
Funding Costs As Percentage of Payroll by Year Group F (Older—2% Decline): Medium Trend Scenario

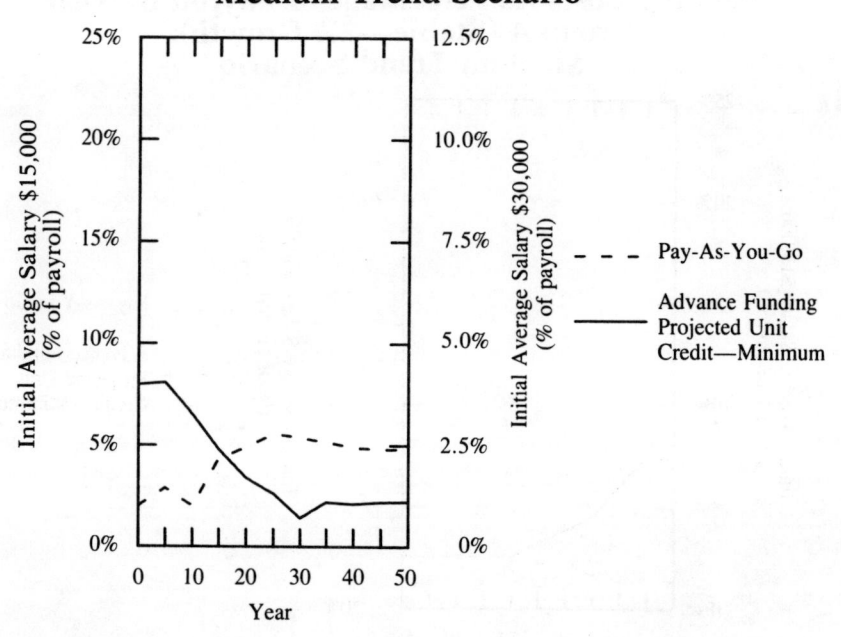

CHART VII.3c
Funding Costs As Percentage of Payroll by Year Group F (Older—7% Decline): Medium Trend Scenario

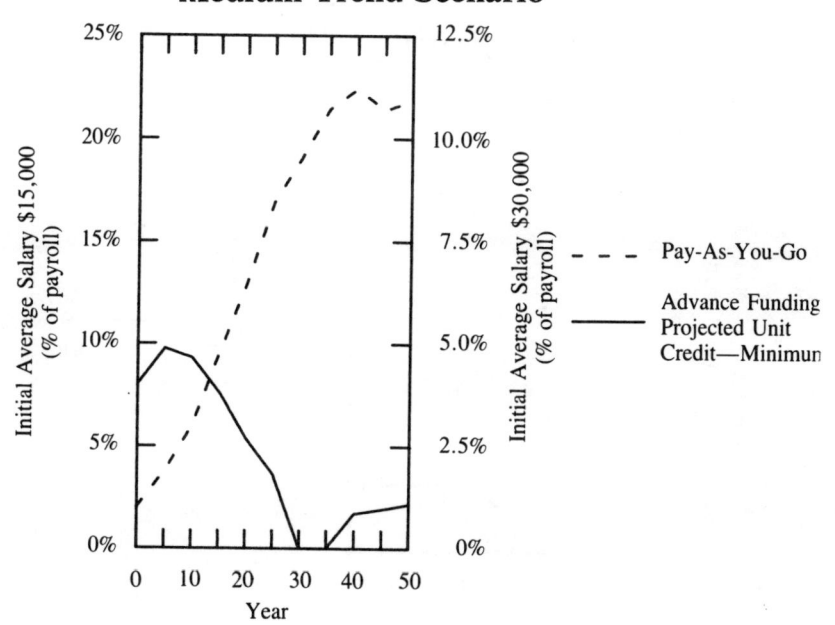

- - - Pay-As-You-Go
——— Advance Funding Projected Unit Credit—Minimum

CHART VII.3d
Funding Costs As Percentage of Payroll by Year Group H (New—2% Growth): Medium Trend Scenario

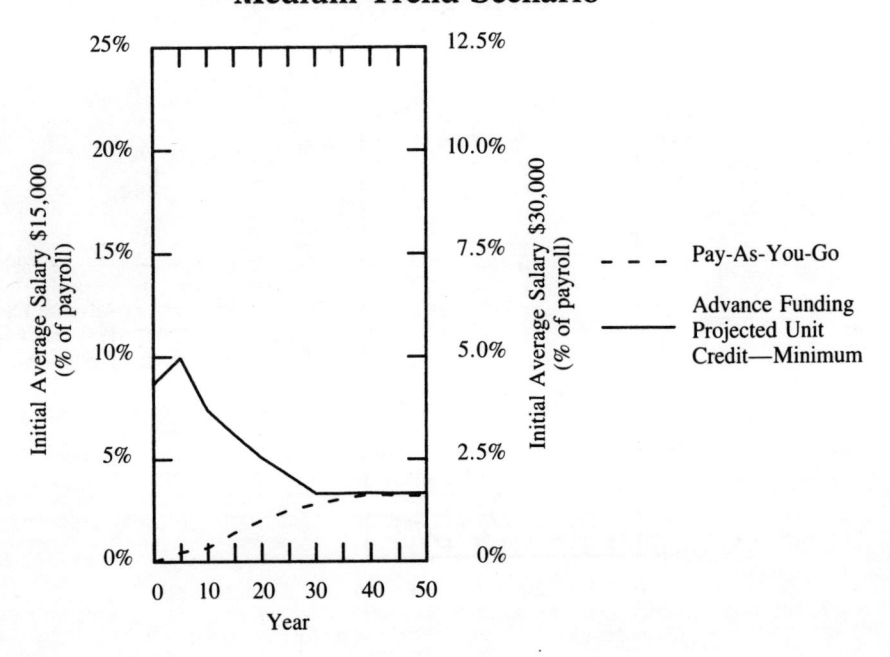

- - - Pay-As-You-Go

—— Advance Funding Projected Unit Credit—Minimum

VIII. Comparison of Funding Adequacy

In this chapter, the funds that accumulate under a range of funding scenarios are analyzed in terms of their adequacy to meet accrued ongoing benefit obligations. The adequacy of these funds to meet the additional benefit obligations that arise when employer operations cease are also examined. Detailed summaries of the benefit liabilities and funding ratios described in this chapter are included in appendices C and D, respectively.

Benefit Liabilities

Chapter IV discussed the concept of benefit accrual as it might apply to retiree medical benefits and illustrated the application of alternative accrual methods to the model groups using closed group projections.

In table VIII.1, the present value of accrued benefits is summarized for Group A based on an open group projection. The accrual method used is ratable accrual from the date of hire to the age of earliest eligibility for retirement (method (4) in table IV.1). Under this method, the liability values for current retirees and vested employees (i.e., those currently eligible to retire) are equal to the present values of future benefits for those populations.

Appendix C includes summaries of the benefit liabilities described above for each of the model groups on an open-group projection basis.

Funding Ratios

A logical measurement of the adequacy of a fund that accumulates under a given funding method is to compare the fund to accrued ongoing benefit obligations. These benefit obligations are defined according to the plan provisions. The benefit accrual method and vesting schedule are used to define the accrued vested benefits and accrued nonvested benefits. The present values of these amounts, assuming ongoing employer operations, offer a measure of accrued ongoing benefit obligations.

Full Funding Methods

In table VIII.2, the fund that accumulates under the Projected Unit Credit—Minimum approach for Group A is compared to the benefit

TABLE VIII.1
Accrued Ongoing Benefit Obligations[a], Group A (Stable), Medium Trend Scenario (millions)

Year	Current Retirees	Vested[b] Employees	Nonvested[b] Employees	Total
0	$ 30	$ 14	$ 41	$ 85
5	46	24	86	156
10	65	42	123	230
15	94	70	160	324
20	139	111	188	438
25	201	151	213	565
30	280	185	233	698
35	411	255	326	992
40	591	351	460	1,402
45	833	494	652	1,979
50	1,170	698	921	2,789

[a]Present value of accrued benefits, based on ratable accrual from date of hire to age of earliest eligibility for retirement.
[b]The terms "vested" and "nonvested" refer here to employees that are currently eligible to retire with benefits and those that are not currently eligible, respectively.

obligations for that group, at five-year intervals. In this comparison, the benefit obligations are equal to the accrued benefit liabilities presented in table VIII.1. For nonvested active workers, the total present value of future benefits is also presented as an alternative measurement.

Fund adequacy is measured in the form of funding ratios. The funding ratio shown for each class of employees is the percentage of the benefit obligation for that class covered by the current fund. The fund is allocated among classes of employees in the following order of priority: first, current retirees; second, vested employees; and third, nonvested employees.

Table VIII.2 indicates that, by the tenth year, the fund exceeds the present value of all future benefits for then-current retirees and for employees that are vested at that time. By the fifteenth year, the fund is also sufficient to cover at least 69 percent of the accrued benefits for nonvested employees, or 32 percent of the total benefits for these employees.

The pattern shown in this funding scenario is fairly typical of that shown by the Full Funding Methods (Entry Age Normal, Projected Unit Credit, and Aggregate) in the funding scenarios studied. Follow-

TABLE VIII.2
Funding Ratios: Full Funding Methods
Group A (Stable), Medium Trend Scenario
Projected Unit Credit—Minimum

Year	Current Retirees	Vested[a] Employees	Nonvested[a] Employees Accrued benefits	Nonvested[a] Employees Total benefits
0	0%	0%	0%	0%
5	100	69	0	0
10	100	100	39	17
15	100	100	69	32
20	100	100	67	32
25	100	100	66	32
30	100	100	65	33
35	100	100	65	32
40	100	100	65	32
45	100	100	65	33
50	100	100	65	33

[a] The terms "vested" and "nonvested" refer here to employees that are currently eligible to retire with benefits and those that are not currently eligible, respectively.

ing is a general description of the funding ratios for these funding methods.

(1) In most cases, the liability for current retirees is funded within five years. The only exceptions to this are in the use of minimum funding standards (i.e., Entry Age Normal or Projected Unit Credit funding with 30-year amortization) for Group F, for which it takes about 10 years to fund current retirees.

(2) Similarly, the present value of future benefits for vested employees is funded within 5 to 10 years in most cases; for Group F, minimum funding takes 10 to 15 years.

(3) After the initial unfunded liability (where applicable) is amortized, the fund is also adequate to cover 50 percent to 100 percent of the accrued benefits for nonvested employees and up to 50 percent of the total future benefits for these employees.

Modified Advance Funding Methods

Table VIII.3 presents the funding ratios generated by the Unprojected Unit Credit—Minimum funding method for Group A. In general, the Unprojected Unit Credit method does not generate a fund adequate to cover liabilities for current retirees; an exception is for Group H (see appendix A), which has only 14 retirees in year 0.

TABLE VIII.3
Funding Ratios: Modified Advance Funding Methods Group A (Stable), Medium Trend Scenario Unprojected Unit Credit—Minimum

Year	Current Retirees	Vested[a] Employees	Nonvested[a] Employees Accrued benefits	Total benefits
0	0%	0%	0%	0%
5	4	0	0	0
10	17	0	0	0
15	32	0	0	0
20	44	0	0	0
25	52	0	0	0
30	59	0	0	0
35	61	0	0	0
40	63	0	0	0
45	66	0	0	0
50	68	0	0	0

[a]The terms "vested" and "nonvested" refer here to employees that are currently eligible to retire with benefits and those that are not currently eligible, respectively.

Table VIII.4 summarizes funding ratios for Group A based on the Unit Credit Method with No Trend or Discount Rate using minimum funding. The general funding pattern of this method is similar to that of the full funding methods. In the early years, when trend exceeds the discount rate under the trend scenarios considered, the Unit Credit Method with No Trend or Discount Rate funds more slowly than the full funding methods. Later, when trend drops below the discount rate, this method generates a higher fund than the full funding methods, exceeding the liability for all accrued benefits.

The funding ratios produced by the Projected Unit Credit Method with Trend Equal to Per Capita GNP Growth Rate, using minimum funding, are presented in table VIII.5. This method accumulates funds more slowly than the full funding methods because those methods are based on a trend assumption greater than 5 percent for the first 15 years or more. After trend drops to 5 percent in these scenarios, this method funds in the same manner as the Projected Unit Credit method.

Funding Ratios: Cessation of Employer Operations

The ratios shown in tables VIII.2 through VIII.5 would change if employer operations ceased at any of the points shown. Chapter IV

TABLE VIII.4
Funding Ratios: Modified Advance Funding Methods Group A (Stable), Medium Trend Scenario, Unit Credit with No Trend or Discount Rate—Minimum

Year	Current Retirees	Vested[a] Employees	Nonvested[a] Employees Accrued benefits	Nonvested[a] Employees Total benefits
0	0%	0%	0%	0%
5	60	0	0	0
10	100	45	0	0
15	100	100	11	5
20	100	100	49	24
25	100	100	100	51
30	100	100	100	79
35	100	100	100	79
40	100	100	100	79
45	100	100	100	79
50	100	100	100	79

[a]The terms "vested" and "nonvested" refer here to employees that are currently eligible to retire with benefits and those that are not currently eligible, respectively.

illustrates the effect of cessation on liabilities for the sample groups. As these liabilities increase due to cessation, the overall funding ratios would decline.

Illustration of Funding Adequacy

The level of liabilities on both an ongoing basis and a cessation basis are illustrated in charts VIII.1a through VIII.4b. In addition, the assets accumulated under advance funding are superimposed on the charts based on the Unit Credit cost method (projected or unprojected as appropriate) reflecting minimum ERISA amortization payments.

TABLE VIII.5
Funding Ratios: Modified Advance Funding Methods Group A (Stable), Medium Trend Scenario Projected Unit Credit with Trend Equal to Per Capita GNP[a]—Minimum

Year	Current Retirees	Vested[b] Employees	Nonvested[b] Employees Accrued benefits	Nonvested[b] Employees Total benefits
0	0%	0%	0%	0%
5	36	0	0	0
10	80	0	0	0
15	100	33	0	0
20	100	77	0	0
25	100	100	15	8
30	100	100	60	30
35	100	100	65	32
40	100	100	65	32
45	100	100	65	33
50	100	100	65	33

[a]Gross National Product.
[b]The terms "vested" and "nonvested" refer here to employees that are currently eligible to retire with benefits and those that are not currently eligible, respectively.

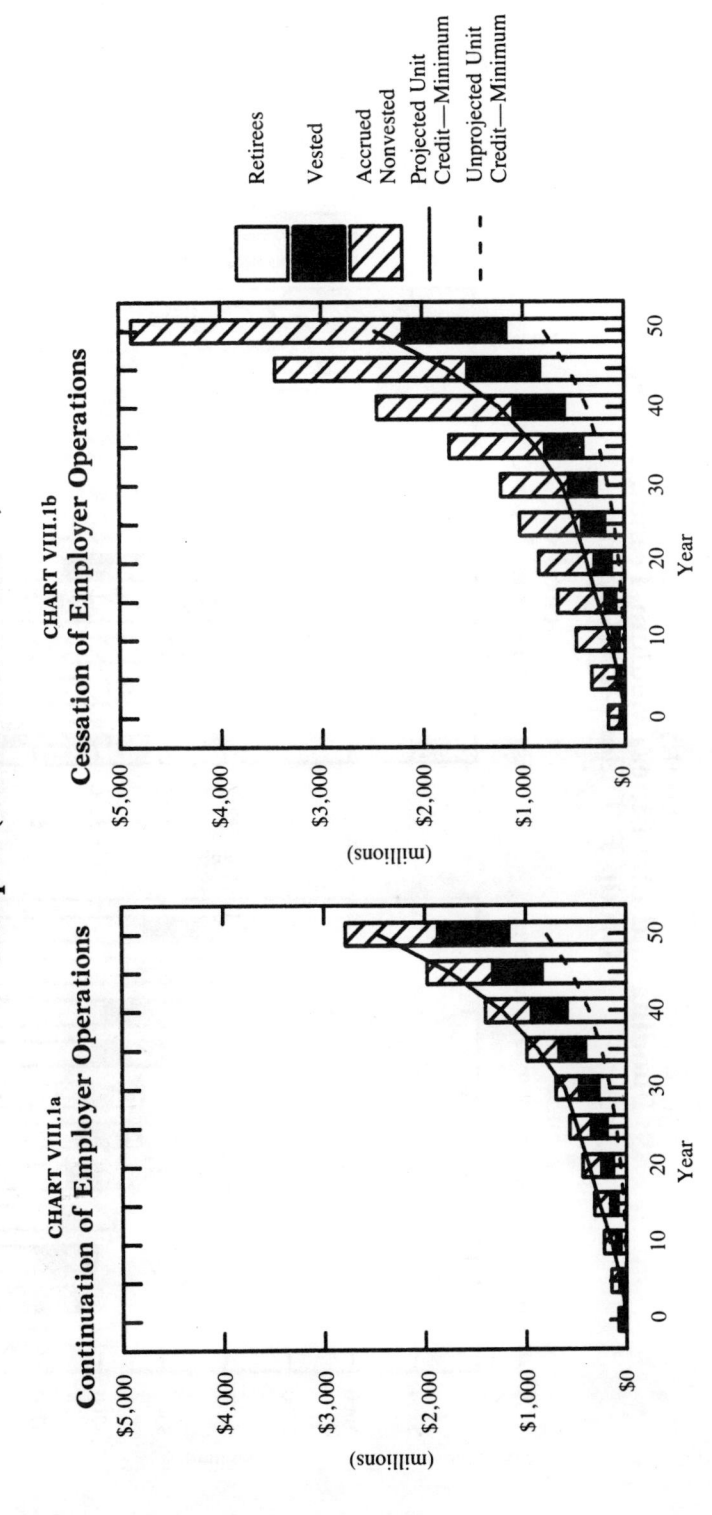

CHART VIII.1
Funding and Liabilities, Medium Trend Scenario
Group A (Stable—2% Growth)

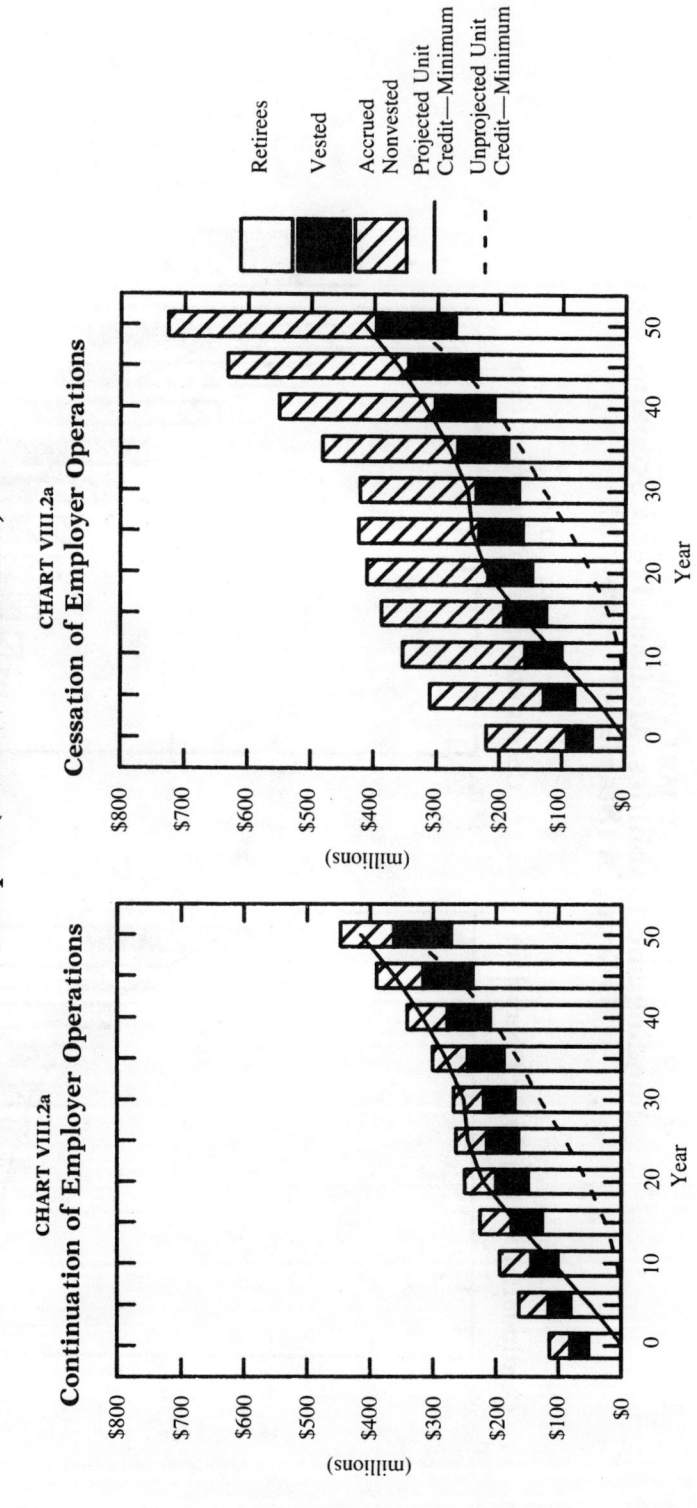

CHART VIII.2
**Funding and Liabilities, Medium Trend Scenario
Group F (Older—2% Decline)**

**CHART VIII.2a
Continuation of Employer Operations**

**CHART VIII.2a
Cessation of Employer Operations**

Legend:
- ☐ Retirees
- ■ Vested
- ▨ Accrued Nonvested
- —— Projected Unit Credit—Minimum
- - - - Unprojected Unit Credit—Minimum

CHART VIII.3
Funding and Liabilities, Medium Trend Scenario
Group F (Older—7% Decline)

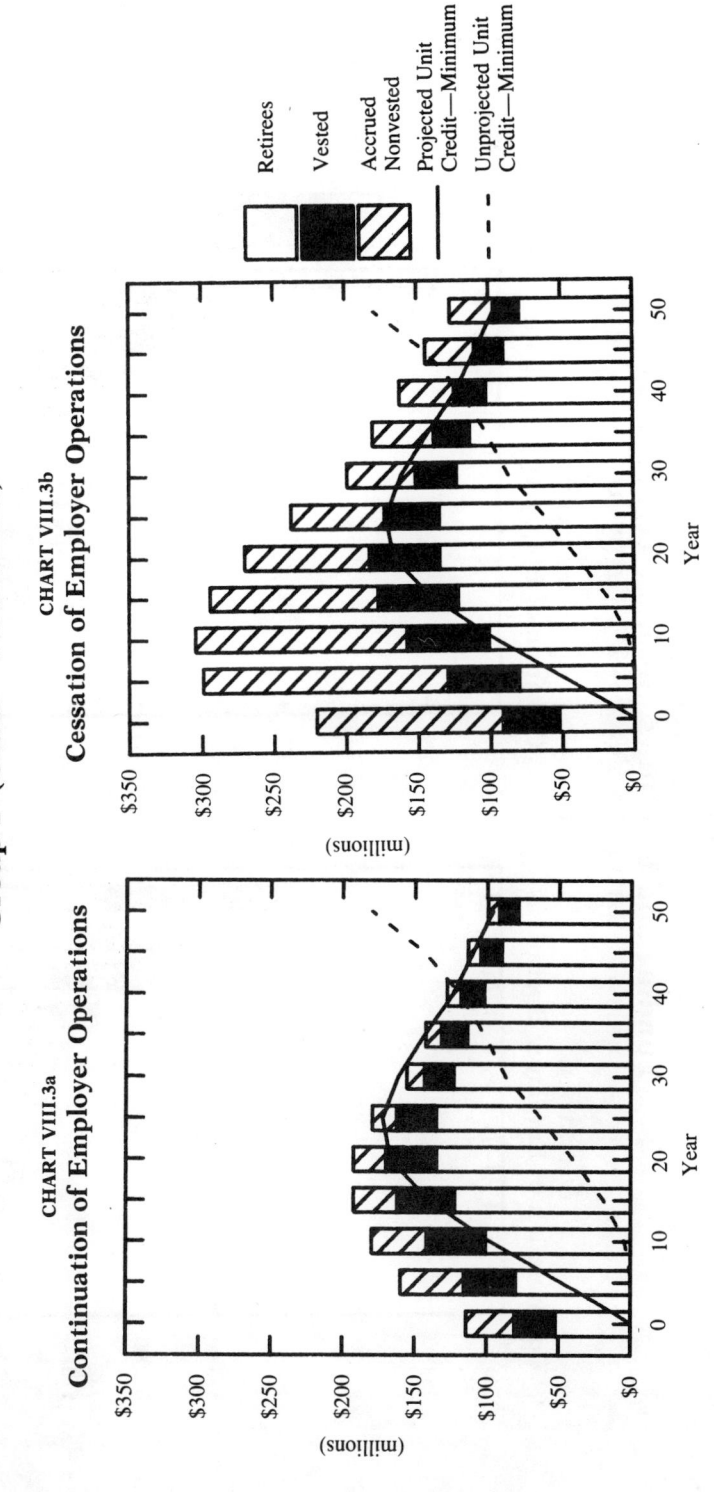

CHART VIII.3a
Continuation of Employer Operations

CHART VIII.3b
Cessation of Employer Operations

CHART VIII.4
Funding and Liabilities, Medium Trend Scenario
Group H (New—2% Growth)

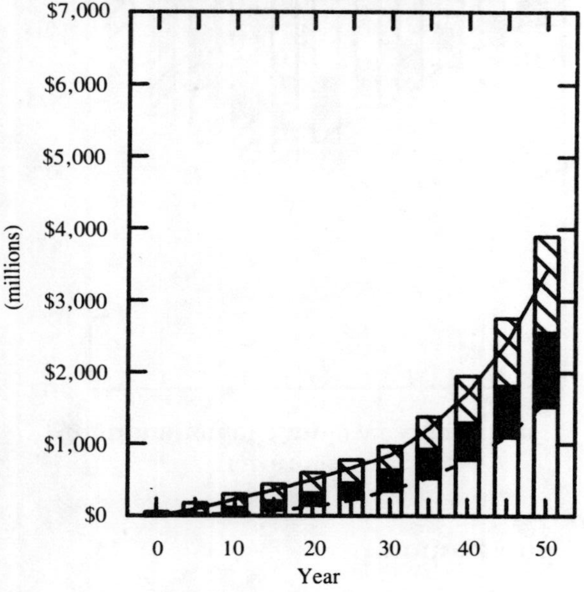

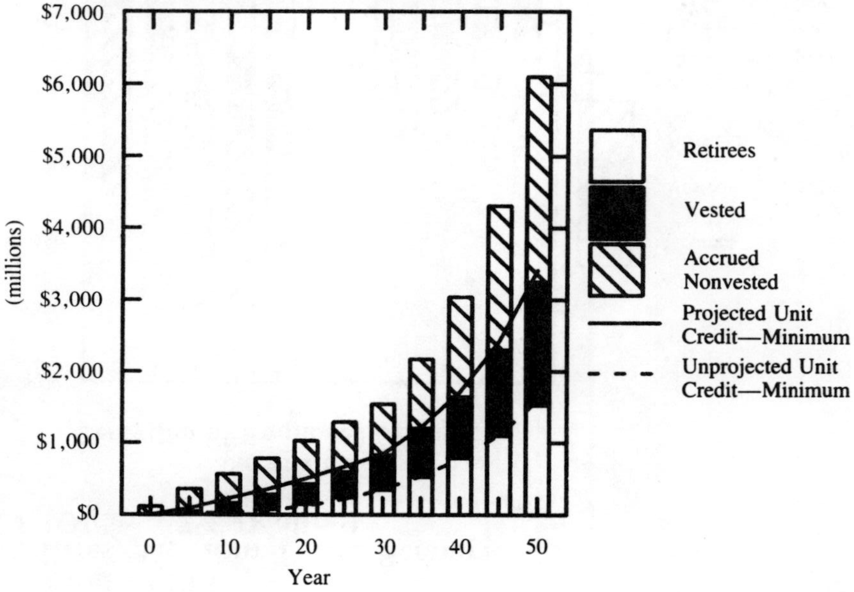

Part Three
Plan Design Issues

IX. Employer Plan Design Alternatives

Recently, employers have been growing more aware of the long-term implications of the benefit promises made to retirees. Employer concerns center on the growing costs of these benefits and the uncertain level of future costs. In addition, recent court decisions indicate that these programs may not be modified or curtailed as easily as had been presumed.

In view of likely Financial Accounting Standards Board (FASB) standards requiring accrual expensing in the near future, and increasing concerns about benefit security, many companies have begun to look at the cost of starting to fund their programs. For employers with a high ratio of retirees to active employees, these costs may be extremely high. For example, chapter VII showed that for Group A (which has one retiree for each six employees) the annual cost to begin advance funding would be $1,000–$2,000 per active employee. For groups with more retirees, or with more generous benefit plans, the cost would be even higher.

While these costs are based on estimates of future benefit payments, actual benefit payments could be higher or lower. Many employers have experienced substantial increases in benefit costs over the last 10 years and are concerned that future costs will be even higher than expected, due to changes in medical technology, Medicare cutbacks, and other unforeseen factors.

As their awareness of these issues increases, employers are likely to look for ways to reduce both the costs and the risks associated with their retiree medical plans; in fact, many have already begun to do this. The types of changes that are being considered fall into two general categories: (1) changes in plan design; and (2) changes in the nature of the promise made to retirees and employees.

This chapter will discuss some of the approaches available to employers in each of these categories. Chapter X will explore some of the issues that must be addressed as employers begin to adopt these changes if advance funding is initiated and vesting standards are enacted.

Changes in Plan Design

In the last decade, most employers have made changes in their medical benefit plans for active employees. These changes have been designed to restrain the rate of increase in employer costs by shifting more costs to employees, reducing unnecessary utilization of services, increasing employee awareness of factors related to good health, or paying reduced fees to providers of medical care.

Some employers have extended these plan changes to current retirees, while others have adopted changes only for future retirees and left benefits intact for current retirees. This latter approach, motivated by concern about potential lawsuits, has resulted in multiple benefit programs and, thus, more costly administration.

A number of factors make it more difficult to change benefits for retirees than for for active employees.

(1) Recent judicial cases have raised questions concerning an employer's right to change retiree benefits after the employee actually retires. Much attention has been focused on promises made verbally during retirement counseling sessions.

(2) For those retirees covered by Medicare, plan changes may have a different effect on expected benefit costs than they will have for active employees.

(3) The retiree population may be quite diverse geographically. This often makes it difficult to adopt provider-specific programs or to communicate complicated benefit changes effectively.

In spite of these factors, there is an increasing trend among employers to modify the design of their retiree medical plans. Following is a brief description of the general types of changes being considered.

Increases in Retiree Cost Sharing

By increasing the level of deductibles and/or coinsurance that a retiree must pay, the employer reduces his or her plan costs directly. In addition, the retiree has a greater incentive to use fewer services or lower-cost services in order to minimize his or her own costs.

For Medicare carve-out plans, the effects of increases in deductibles and coinsurance for retirees over age 65 will vary, depending on how the program coordinates with Medicare. For example, a plan that relies on the traditional coordination of benefits provision, thereby filling in Medicare deductibles and coinsurance, may be only slightly affected. On the other hand, a plan that pays the difference between plan benefits and the amount of benefits paid by Medicare will be directly affected.

Increases in Retiree Contributions

Some employers are increasing annually the level of contributions payable by employees or retirees in order to be eligible for coverage.

Such increases may be proportional to increases in employer costs, or may even be higher, as is often the case in flexible benefit plans. Employer costs are reduced directly, due to the effect of retiree contributions, and may also be lowered due to declines in participation, as some retirees choose to obtain coverage elsewhere rather than pay the higher contribution.

Some employers are hesitant to increase contributions for current retirees for fear of legal action, and therefore freeze the level of contribution at the time of retirement. As shown in chapter III, employer costs may be increased substantially due to such freezes; for a plan where retirees contribute 50 percent of the cost of coverage, employer costs would be 60 percent higher if these contributions were frozen at retirement.

Utilization Management Programs

As broadly defined, utilization management programs include a wide array of services and techniques designed to reduce unnecessary utilization of medical care services. Many of these programs are more difficult to apply to retirees, and some cannot, as a practical matter, be applied to Medicare beneficiaries.

Following are some considerations regarding the extension of utilization management programs to retirees.

(1) For retirees enrolled in Medicare, it is difficult to apply utilization review criteria more stringent than those applied by the Medicare program, because retirees would be subject to two different sets of conditions. In fact, some employer plans currently cover services not approved for payment under Medicare, and in effect pay such claims as regular benefits rather than Medicare carve-out benefits.

(2) Some programs require the covered employee or retiree to take positive action before receiving certain services, such as precertification for hospital admission or second opinions for certain surgical procedures. These requirements often lead to confusion on the part of the employee or retiree, perhaps leaving him or her fully liable for payment of claims. These problems tend to be even greater for a retiree population that may not have direct access to employer information services.

(3) One area that may offer significant opportunity for savings in retiree benefit costs is that of prescription drugs. Under a typical Medicare carve-out plan, outpatient drugs may account for 25 to 40 percent of total costs. Generic equivalent, preferred pharmacy, or mail-order programs are increasingly utilized by employers to reduce their costs of prescription drug coverage.

Multiple Options

Multiple option programs offer each employee a choice of benefit plans, where he or she may choose to accept limitations on the choice of providers or may pay a higher contribution in return for more extensive benefit coverage.

Most of these programs involve one or more options that restrict employee selection of hospitals and physicians to those that are participating in the program—these are called health maintenance organizations (HMOs) or preferred provider organizations (PPOs). The objective of such programs is to encourage employee enrollment in program options that offer potential for reducing utilization of services or that offer fee discounts, thus reducing employer costs overall.

Some employers have begun to offer these options to retirees, particularly those under age 65. However, for retirees that have moved away from the employer's geographic area or live part of the year in another location, HMO and PPO options often are not practical. As mentioned earlier, programs that limit retiree use of medical care are difficult to apply to those enrolled in Medicare.

Variation in Retiree Benefits by Length of Service

Currently, most plans require a minimum length of service, such as 10 years, in order for retirees to receive medical benefits. Frequently the required service period is identical to the minimum required for pension benefits. Employees with this minimum level of service receive the full medical benefit at retirement—the same level of benefits as longer-service employees.

One approach to reducing future benefit costs is to lengthen the service requirement for full benefits; employees not meeting this longer requirement would then be eligible to receive a benefit for which the employer would pay only a portion of the cost and the retiree would be required to pay the balance as an annual contribution. For example, assume the plan provides full coverage for 30 years of service with reduced benefits available for 10 years of service. The employee that retires with 10 years of service might be entitled to receive the benefit from the employer if he or she pays two-thirds of the cost.

Changes in the Nature of Benefit Commitments

While all of the plan design changes outlined above may help to limit increases in benefit plan costs, overall program costs are still increasing for most employers. The projected future costs of retiree medical plans and the uncertainty regarding these costs may lead more employers to consider changing the nature of the promise they make to future retirees.

Most employers believe they have the right to reduce or eliminate benefits for future generations of retirees. Concern over the security of these benefits, however, has led policymakers to discuss legislation aimed at protecting retirees' rights to future benefits through funding and vesting requirements.

If faced with a clear requirement to guarantee continuation of current benefit coverage for future retirees, or even for current retirees, some employers might choose instead to establish the level of expenditure for such benefits, either as a fixed rate of contribution or as a specific dollar benefit. Instead of receiving a specified level of medical coverage paid for by the employer, the retiree would receive a dollar benefit similar to a pension. This dollar amount would be applied toward the purchase of medical coverage, with the retiree responsible for contributing whatever amount is required to provide the difference between the full cost of the coverage and the specific dollar amount provided by the employer.

Employers choosing to change the nature of benefit commitments to retirees in this manner must decide to whom such changes will apply. This decision will depend on what promises have been made to current retirees and employees, both written and verbal. Future changes might be limited, for example, to those employees not currently eligible to retire or to those that are a certain number of years away from eligibility. In any case, a transition plan must be developed so that changes can be adequately communicated and implemented smoothly and fairly.

There are two general approaches that might be considered by employers desiring to limit the nature of the medical benefit guarantees offered to future retirees.

Defined Dollar Benefit

Under this approach, the employer would guarantee an annual retirement benefit in dollar terms, to be used to purchase medical coverage for the retiree. This benefit structure would be similar to that of a defined benefit pension plan.

Defined Contribution

Alternatively, the employer might choose to guarantee an annual contribution during the period of active employment, similar to a defined contribution pension plan, to provide medical coverage during retirement. These contributions, accumulated with interest, would be available to the employee at retirement to apply toward the purchase of medical coverage.

Under both approaches, the employer terminates the current type of open-ended agreement to provide coverage. Instead, future benefits would be defined in terms of dollars; to the extent that the dollar benefit falls short of meeting the cost of coverage during retirement, the retiree would pay the additional cost unless he or she has other coverage available.

These two approaches are discussed further in chapter X.

X. Changes in Employer Commitments: Funding and Vesting Implications

Chapter IX described several approaches that might be taken by employers to reduce the cost of providing retiree medical benefits, two of which involve a fundamental change in the nature of the benefit commitment. These approaches, defined dollar benefit plans and defined contribution plans, would promise to the employee a certain level of expenditure by the company on retiree medical benefits, rather than promise a certain level of medical care coverage.

Such approaches have also been proposed by policymakers as alternative methods for funding retiree medical benefits. The similarity of these approaches to pensions may offer the opportunity to apply existing funding and vesting standards, thus simplifying the regulation of retiree medical benefits in a tax-preferred funding environment (i.e., an environment in which advance funding of retiree medical benefits is encouraged through favorable tax treatment of funding contributions).

This chapter will consider the implications of using these alternative approaches to fund retiree medical benefit programs. What features would be required under these methods to provide sound benefit programs, with advance funding and vesting of benefits prior to retirement? There are a number of issues that would need to be resolved before this question could be answered completely; the following discussion outlines some of these issues.

Benefit Adequacy

Each of these approaches shifts to the retiree the risk that funds available under the plan will be inadequate to meet future costs of medical care coverage. The retiree must absorb any differences between such costs and the funds available to him or her under the benefit formula.

The defined dollar or defined contribution benefit formula should reflect the employer's objectives regarding benefit adequacy for various classes of employees. Table X.1 summarizes the present value of future medical benefits for an individual retiring today at selected ages. These values are based on the per capita plan costs used in this study, assuming an 8 percent annual medical trend.

TABLE X.1
Present Value of Future Medical Benefits for an Individual Retiring Today[a]

Age at Retirement (male retiree)	Single	Married
55	$15,000	$31,000
60	11,000	23,000
65	6,000	14,000

[a]Based on sample benefit plan used in this study; see table III.2 for adjustments to reflect higher levels of coverage.

As shown, the present value of future benefits ranges from $6,000 for a single retiree at age 65 to $31,000 for a married retiree at age 55. Therefore, a benefit formula that provides adequate funds for coverage for an unmarried individual retiring at age 65 would produce inadequate funds for an employee that is married or is retiring at a younger age, unless special supplements were offered.

Table X.2 summarizes the level dollar contribution that would be required, under a defined contribution plan established today, to fully fund the medical benefits shown in table X.1 for an individual hired today at age 35 or 45 and retiring in the future at selected ages. The required contribution varies significantly by age at retirement; for an employee retiring at age 55, the required contribution would be three times as high as it would be if he or she continued to work to age 65.

TABLE X.2
Annual Level Dollar Contribution Required to Fully Fund Postretirement Medical Benefits[a]

Age at Hire (male retiree)	Age at Retirement	Single	Married
35	55	$1,700	$3,500
	60	1,200	2,500
	65	600	1,500
45	55	2,300	4,800
	60	1,400	2,900
	65	700	1,600

[a]Reflects sample benefit plan used in this study.

This comparison illustrates the need to consider what level of funding is desired for various classes of employees. Some of the issues to be considered by an employer in developing a defined benefit or defined contribution benefit formula to fund retiree medical benefits are discussed below.

Length of Service

To what extent will the plan reward long-service employees more than short-service employees? A formula that varies benefits by length of service, such as a defined contribution plan, might be targeted to produce benefits for certain long-service employees (however defined) that are likely to be adequate to cover the costs of medical coverage. Short-service employees, then, would find their benefits falling short of covering these costs.

On the other hand, if the employer wishes to provide comparable benefits for all employees provided they meet some minimum service requirements, a defined dollar benefit formula could be used, with benefit units that are not a function of years of service.

Early Vesting

Should benefits be made available to employees that do not retire from the company? Currently, benefits under most retiree medical plans do not vest until the employee is eligible for retirement. If tax-preferred funding of these benefits were to be offered in the future, however, there might also be requirements that benefits vest prior to retirement, similar to current requirements for pension benefits. If early vesting is granted, formulas for benefit accrual would also be required. If vesting is provided, how would an employee that has a vested benefit under two or more company plans be treated? Would benefits be portable?

Early Retirement Subsidies

Should the higher medical benefit costs associated with early retirement be subsidized by the employer? An employer that wants to subsidize these early retirement benefits may need to provide a supplemental benefit to employees retiring prior to age 65 for this purpose. This is very difficult to do under a defined contribution plan without providing excessive benefits to those who wait until age 65 or later to retire. For example, if these contributions were based on the assumption that the employee would retire at, say, age 60, then the accumulated fund would tend to be inadequate if he or she retired at age 55, and excessive if he or she retired at age 65. For this reason, it would be difficult to develop a defined contribution benefit formula that would produce reasonably adequate funding for a large majority of retirees without special supplements.

Dependent Coverage Subsidies

Should the additional cost of spouse and dependent coverage be subsidized? If so, the plan could include a supplemental benefit payable to retirees that have spouses and dependents at the time of retirement. Again, this is difficult to accomplish in a defined contribution arrangement, since employees married during active employment may be divorced or widowed at retirement while others may be single until shortly before retirement.

The employer's objectives regarding these issues and others will determine what type of benefit formula is appropriate. Because the cost of retiree medical coverage does not vary with service or salary, the formula must either provide benefits on a per capita basis or, alternatively, provide benefits to some retirees that are inadequate to purchase the level of coverage made available to others.

In a defined contribution plan, a "target benefit plan" approach could be used to determine for each employee the level of annual contribution that would produce the desired benefit at retirement. In other words, a higher contribution would be made for an employee hired at age 40 than for an employee hired at age 30.

A defined dollar benefit formula could be designed to produce an annual dollar benefit that would approximate the year-to-year pattern of the expected cost of coverage. Table X.3 illustrates the annual per capita cost of coverage at selected future ages for an individual retiring today at age 55. These costs increase annually due to the effects of medical cost trends and the progression of average costs by age. The costs drop at age 65, when Medicare becomes effective.

A defined dollar benefit that would match this annual cost of coverage would be one that increased in each year of retirement to reflect increasing medical costs with advancing age and included a temporary supplement at early retirement payable until age 65. In addition, a supplemental benefit would be required for retirees with spouses or dependents if this coverage also were to be funded.

The costs in table X.3 will be higher for an individual retiring in future years, due to the trend in medical care costs. Therefore, another requirement of a defined benefit formula, if it were to provide adequate benefits for most retirees, would be that the benefit payable at each age increase every year based on the expected trend.

TABLE X.3
Illustrative Future Annual Per Capita Costs for Individual Retiring Today at Age 55

		Married Retiree	
Age	Single Retiree	Spouse	Retiree and spouse
55	$ 781	$ 703	$1,484
57	958	862	1,820
59	1,173	1,056	2,229
61	1,438	1,294	2,732
63	1,762	1,586	3,348
65	540	486	1,026
67	662	596	1,258
69	811	730	1,541
71	994	895	1,889
73	1,219	1,097	2,316
75	1,492	1,343	2,835

In the absence of such built-in calendar year increases, the defined dollar benefit plan might be analogous to a negotiated hourly pension plan, in which a fixed benefit is written into the plan, then changed through bargaining to reflect changing economic conditions. It should be noted that many of these pension plans, which tend to be found in declining industries, are currently inadequately funded because of the failure to anticipate in funding the level of future benefit increases that will be negotiated.

If a similar approach were taken in funding for retiree medical benefits, the adequacy of the funds accumulated would be comparable to the adequacy of a plan funded with the Unprojected Unit Credit method. As indicated in chapter VIII, this method does not accumulate adequate funds to provide full benefit security for current retirees in the event of a curtailment of contributions, and provides nothing for employees not yet retired.

Vesting and Portability

Under defined contribution and defined benefit approaches, an important issue that must be addressed is the nature of the retiree's "vested" right. Is the retiree vested in a specific dollar benefit, or in the right to apply this benefit to purchase medical coverage?

If the retiree were vested in the dollar benefit, then it would be possible to apply pension-type vesting and accrual formulas to this benefit. If an employee were to vest in these benefits prior to eligibility for retirement and leave service prior to retirement age, the fully vested benefit could be made available to him or her at the time of retirement. Alternatively, the employee might have the option of rolling over the dollar benefit to the new employer's plan or a separate account designated for this purpose.

If the employee is vested in the dollar benefit, this would also imply that he or she could choose to take the funds and not necessarily use them to purchase medical coverage. This might lead to selection problems for employers offering retirees the option to purchase coverage through a group plan.

If vesting is provided, it is difficult to define the nature of the vested right to spouse or dependent coverage. For example, if a fully vested employee leaves prior to retirement, does the employee have a right to a spouse benefit at retirement if he or she is married at termination of employment? If so, what happens if he or she is not married at the time of retirement—would this spouse benefit constitute a windfall to the single employee? Alternatively, it is possible that an employee that was not married at the time of vesting would be married at the time of retirement; is that employee entitled to spouse coverage?

Other questions arise if the retiree is considered to be vested only in the right to apply the available funds toward the purchase of medical coverage. In this situation, what would happen if the retiree chose not to make the contribution required to purchase coverage? Would the employee forfeit the right to the funds that had been accumulated in his or her name? Also, if the employee is fully vested in this right, and then changes employers, does this right transfer to the new employer program?

These are issues that could be addressed in a number of ways. Until some of these basic questions are answered, however, it is difficult to identify optimal benefit designs, or to structure programs for providing retiree medical coverage through defined dollar benefit or defined contribution plans.

Retiree Coverage Options

When funds are made available to the retiree for the purchase of medical coverage, the employer may want to offer the retiree certain options for purchasing the coverage through a group plan. In a tax-preferred funding environment, a scenario such as the following might be appropriate.

(1) Any employer that so chooses could offer retirees the option to purchase coverage through an employer plan. An important consideration under such an approach would be the determination of the cost of coverage for each retiree.

(2) To avoid severe adverse selection problems, it would be necessary to devise a risk classification system that would correspond roughly to the actual cost of coverage. In other words, retirees age 65 should be charged less for coverage than retirees age 60, who do not have Medicare coverage. Otherwise, the cost of coverage would appear high for the retiree age 65, and he or she may choose to purchase coverage elsewhere. As a result, only those retirees that found the rate attractive (e.g., those without Medicare coverage) would participate, and the average rates charged to them would ultimately prove to be inadequate.

(3) Alternatively, an employer might want to offer retirees a number of coverage options. There might be a lower-cost plan, available to those retirees that have a lower dollar benefit available for purchase of coverage. Again, the potential problems of adverse selection would require a careful construction of the basis for assessing the cost of coverage to each retiree.

(4) For those retirees choosing not to purchase coverage through an employer plan, or for those whose employers do not offer such a plan, the dollar benefit could be used to purchase coverage elsewhere. For example, a retiree might have the option of purchasing coverage from a previous employer or through the spouse's employer, or of purchasing an individual policy.

(5) Options available to retirees could be structured to produce incentives for buying the employer plan. For example, a retiree might be allowed to apply the dollar benefit toward the employer plan on a pretax basis, but would be taxed if he or she chose to withdraw the funds and purchase coverage elsewhere. Alternatively, the tax preference could be extended to certain "qualified" plan options, such as other qualified employer programs, and perhaps certain qualified plans offered by designated carriers.

(6) Another option that might be available to the retiree choosing not to purchase medical coverage would be a spending account approach. The dollar amount of his or her benefit could be applied toward medical claims, and perhaps to purchase long-term care services. Once the fund was exhausted, however, the retiree would have no remaining benefits under the plan.

At the present time, these approaches to providing retiree medical benefits are not common. If defined dollar benefit and/or defined contribution plans were to be encouraged in the future through legislation, programs to facilitate the purchase of coverage by retirees would need to be developed.

Employee Funding Options

Regardless of the approach taken to fund benefits, many employers will tend to provide a relatively smaller portion of the retiree medical coverage to future retirees than they have in the past. This is a likely result of the continually increasing costs of providing such coverage.

Therefore, the individual employee and retiree will be forced to share a greater burden of the cost of medical care coverage during retirement. For this reason, employers might want to offer employees the option of contributing funds during their working years to be applied toward the purchase of medical care coverage during retirement. To encourage such employee funding, employers might choose to match employee contributions on a limited basis; such matching could provide an alternative application of employer contributions toward medical coverage.

There is growing concern about the need for vehicles to fund coverage for long-term care, i.e., custodial care for retirees, which is not covered under a typical medical insurance plan. The type of employee funding options described above could also be made available to allow and encourage employees to begin funding for such long-term care benefits during their working lifetimes.

Appendix A
Description of Major Assumptions

The American Academy of Actuaries Committee on Pension Actuarial Principles and Practices produced the study *Pension Cost Method Analysis*, which analyzed costs and liabilities for 10 participant groups under various actuarial cost methods.[1] The purpose of the analysis was to provide information useful to the Financial Accounting Standards Board (FASB) in its development of procedures for accounting for pension plan costs and liabilities. Participant data was selected from actual plans. To facilitate comparisons of emerging costs and liabilities, all groups were prorated to an active employee group of 10,000 participants.

Three participant groups—A, F, and H—were selected for use in this study. They are characterized in the Academy report as follows:

(1) **A: Stable Group**—This represents a reasonably mature and stable group that is projected to continue to grow. It is typical of many large companies.

(2) **F: Older, Declining Group**—This represents an older, mature group that is gradually declining. Turnover is high at all ages and durations of employment.

(3) **H: New Group**—This is a new group typical of emerging high-technology companies. The hypothetical company has been in business approximately five years. Most employees have been hired since that time. It was initially formed by transferring employees from other divisions of the parent. The average age at employment is high and expected to remain high because of the skill and experience required in the company's business. Turnover is relatively high, particularly at younger ages and short service durations.

Active participant data for each of these groups is summarized in tables A.1 through A.3. Active participants are assumed to be equally divided between males and females within each age and service classification. Salaries used in the Academy study have been increased to reflect an initial valuation date of January 1, 1987, compared with January 1, 1984, in the Academy study. The wage increase assumed during the interim period is proportionate to the change recorded by

---

[1] American Academy of Actuaries, *Pension Cost Method Analysis* (Washington, DC: American Adacemy of Actuaries, 1985).

the Social Security Administration in average national earnings from 1982 to 1985.

Initial retiree, spouse, and surviving spouse populations (from the Academy study) have been distributed based on the retirement population of a major U.S. employer. Retirees are assumed to be equally divided between males and females at each age. Surviving spouses are assumed to be two-thirds females and one-third males. Distributions of these populations by age are included in tables A.4 through A.6.

TABLE A.1
Participant Data—Active Employees: Group A
Age and Years of Continuous Service

Years of Credited Service

Attained Age	0.5	1.5	3.0	7.0	12.0	17.0	22.0	27.0	32.0	37.0	40.0	Total
22	0	492	1,041	106	0	0	0	0	0	0	0	1,639
27	0	258	1,224	611	50	0	0	0	0	0	0	2,143
32	6	150	528	589	264	28	0	0	0	0	0	1,565
37	3	103	361	386	314	106	3	0	0	0	0	1,276
42	0	72	225	200	147	142	64	17	0	0	0	867
47	0	31	161	167	94	78	83	58	17	0	0	689
52	0	56	106	128	108	103	25	42	33	6	0	607
57	0	28	114	172	125	78	36	31	36	28	6	654
62	0	6	61	81	131	72	31	33	17	14	17	463
67	0	0	0	19	36	14	11	0	3	6	8	97
Total	9	1,196	3,821	2,459	1,269	621	253	181	106	54	31	10,000

TABLE A.2
Participant Data—Active Employees: Group F
Age and Years of Continuous Service

Attained Age	\multicolumn{9}{c}{Years of Credited Service}	
	0.5	1.5	3.0	7.0	12.0	17.0	22.0	27.0	32.0	37.0	40.0	Total
22	0	395	544	0	0	0	0	0	0	0	0	939
27	0	325	717	518	35	0	0	0	0	0	0	1,595
32	0	123	448	527	316	53	0	0	0	0	0	1,467
37	0	79	334	500	263	202	0	0	0	0	0	1,378
42	0	44	176	395	149	211	123	0	0	0	0	1,098
47	0	61	167	140	105	114	193	158	18	0	0	956
52	0	53	105	158	97	79	114	114	132	26	0	878
57	0	18	44	88	79	114	70	140	140	167	18	878
62	0	0	18	79	97	97	132	97	61	88	79	748
67	0	0	0	0	18	9	9	18	9	0	0	63
Total	0	1,098	2,553	2,405	1,159	879	641	527	360	281	97	10,000

TABLE A.3
Participant Data—Active Employees: Group H
Age and Years of Continuous Service

Attained Age	\multicolumn{10}{c}{Years of Credited Service}	
	0.5	1.5	3.0	7.0	12.0	17.0	22.0	27.0	32.0	37.0	40.0	Total
22	0	629	233	44	0	0	0	0	0	0	0	906
27	0	899	862	352	0	0	0	0	0	0	0	2,113
32	0	440	484	252	6	0	0	0	0	0	0	1,182
37	0	333	484	314	0	0	6	0	0	0	0	1,137
42	0	302	528	377	0	38	13	0	0	0	0	1,258
47	0	220	484	384	6	31	19	6	0	0	0	1,150
52	0	164	459	333	13	19	57	13	0	0	0	1,058
57	0	138	283	264	13	13	13	0	0	0	0	724
62	0	25	233	195	0	0	6	0	0	0	0	459
67	0	0	0	13	0	0	0	0	0	0	0	13
Total	0	3,150	4,050	2,528	38	101	114	19	0	0	0	10,000

TABLE A.4
Participant Data—Inactive Participants: Group A

	Male Retirees and Their Spouses				Female Retirees and Their Spouses		
Attained age	Number of retirees	Spouse age	Number of spouses	Attained age	Number of retirees	Spouse age	Number of spouses
55	17	52	14	55	18	58	13
56	21	53	17	56	21	59	15
57	25	54	20	57	23	60	16
58	28	55	23	58	24	61	16
59	35	56	28	59	26	62	17
60	42	57	34	60	27	63	18
61	45	58	36	61	28	64	18
62	50	59	40	62	29	65	18
63	46	60	36	63	28	66	17
64	41	61	32	64	30	67	18
65	41	62	32	65	32	68	19
66	36	63	28	66	31	69	18
67	30	64	23	67	30	70	16
68	26	65	20	68	26	71	14
69	23	66	18	69	24	72	12
70	20	67	15	70	27	73	13
71	19	68	14	71	31	74	14
72	20	69	15	72	32	75	13
73	21	70	16	73	34	76	13
74	21	71	15	74	32	77	11

75	22	72	16	75	32	78	10
76	22	73	15	76	30	79	9
77	21	74	14	77	26	80	7
78	20	75	13	78	24	81	6
79	18	76	12	79	22	82	4
80	16	77	10	80	19	83	3
81	13	78	8	81	17	84	2
82	12	79	7	82	13	85	2
83	10	80	6	83	12	86	1
84	7	81	4	84	9	87	1
85	6	82	3	85	8	88	1
86	5	83	3	86	6	89	0
87	4	84	2	87	6	90	0
88	3	85	1	88	4	91	0
89	2	86	1	89	4	92	0
90	2	87	1	90	3	93	0
91	1	88	0	91	2	94	0
92	1	89	0	92	1	95	0
93	1	90	0	93	1	96	0
94	1	91	0	94	1	97	0
95	0	92	0	95	1	98	0
96	0	93	0	96	0	99	0
97	0	94	0	97	0	100	0
98	0	95	0	98	0	101	0
99	0	96	0	99	0	102	0
100	0	97	0	100	0	103	0
Total	794		592		794		355

(continued)

TABLE A.4 (continued)

| Male Surviving Spouses || Female Surviving Spouses ||
Attained age	Number	Attained age	Number
58	5	52	2
59	6	53	3
60	7	54	4
61	8	55	5
62	8	56	6
63	9	57	7
64	7	58	7
65	7	59	8
66	6	60	8
67	5	61	8
68	4	62	9
69	4	63	9
70	3	64	9
71	3	65	10
72	3	66	9
73	4	67	9
74	3	68	8
75	4	69	7
76	4	70	8
77	4	71	9
78	3	72	10
79	3	73	10
80	3	74	10

81	2	75	10
82	2	76	9
83	2	77	8
84	1	78	7
85	1	79	7
86	1	80	6
87	1	81	5
88	1	82	4
89	0	83	4
90	0	84	3
91	0	85	2
92	0	86	2
93	0	87	2
94	0	88	1
95	0	89	1
96	0	90	1
97	0	91	1
98	0	92	0
99	0	93	0
100	0	94	0
101	0	95	0
102	0	96	0
103	0	97	0
Total	124		248

TABLE A.5
Participant Data—Inactive Participants: Group F

	Male Retirees and Their Spouses				Female Retirees and Their Spouses			
Attained age	Number of retirees	Spouse age	Number of spouses	Attained age	Number of retirees	Spouse age	Number of spouses
55	33	52	27	55	35	58	25
56	41	53	33	56	41	59	29
57	48	54	39	57	43	60	30
58	54	55	44	58	46	61	32
59	66	56	53	59	49	62	33
60	80	57	64	60	51	63	34
61	87	58	69	61	53	64	34
62	94	59	75	62	55	65	35
63	89	60	71	63	54	66	33
64	78	61	62	64	55	67	33
65	77	62	61	65	63	68	37
66	69	63	54	66	61	69	34
67	57	64	45	67	58	70	31
68	50	65	39	68	49	71	26
69	44	66	34	69	46	72	23
70	38	67	29	70	52	73	24
71	36	68	27	71	59	74	26
72	37	69	28	72	60	75	25
73	40	70	30	73	64	76	24
74	39	71	28	74	62	77	22

75	42	72	30	75	60	78	19
76	42	73	29	76	56	79	16
77	41	74	28	77	50	80	13
78	38	75	25	78	45	81	10
79	35	76	23	79	42	82	8
80	30	77	19	80	37	83	6
81	25	78	16	81	32	84	4
82	22	79	13	82	26	85	3
83	19	80	11	83	23	86	2
84	14	81	8	84	18	87	2
85	12	82	6	85	15	88	1
86	9	83	5	86	12	89	1
87	7	84	3	87	11	90	1
88	6	85	3	88	9	91	1
89	5	86	2	89	7	92	0
90	3	87	1	90	5	93	0
91	3	88	1	91	4	94	0
92	2	89	1	92	3	95	0
93	1	90	0	93	2	96	0
94	1	91	0	94	1	97	0
95	1	92	0	95	1	98	0
96	1	93	0	96	1	99	0
97	0	94	0	97	0	100	0
98	0	95	0	98	0	101	0
99	0	96	0	99	0	102	0
100	0	97	0	100	0	103	0
Total	1,516		1,136		1,516		677

(continued)

TABLE A.5 (continued)

| Male Surviving Spouses || Female Surviving Spouses ||
Attained age	Number	Attained age	Number
58	6	52	3
59	7	53	4
60	9	54	5
61	10	55	8
62	11	56	9
63	10	57	10
64	9	58	10
65	9	59	11
66	8	60	12
67	6	61	13
68	5	62	12
69	4	63	12
70	4	64	12
71	4	65	14
72	5	66	13
73	5	67	13
74	5	68	11
75	5	69	10
76	5	70	11
77	5	71	13
78	5	72	13
79	4	73	14
80	4	74	14

81	3	75	13
82	3	76	13
83	2	77	11
84	2	78	10
85	1	79	9
86	1	80	8
87	1	81	7
88	1	82	6
89	1	83	5
90	0	84	4
91	0	85	3
92	0	86	3
93	0	87	2
94	0	88	2
95	0	89	2
96	0	90	1
97	0	91	1
98	0	92	1
99	0	93	0
100	0	94	0
101	5	95	0
102	5	96	0
103	5	97	0
Total	175		348

TABLE A.6
Participant Data—Inactive Participants: Group H

Male Retirees and Their Spouses				Female Retirees and Their Spouses			
Attained age	Number of retirees	Spouse age	Number of spouses	Attained age	Number of retirees	Spouse age	Number of spouses
55	0	52	0	55	0	58	0
56	0	53	0	56	0	59	0
57	0	54	0	57	0	60	0
58	0	55	0	58	0	61	0
59	0	56	0	59	0	62	0
60	0	57	0	60	0	63	0
61	0	58	0	61	0	64	0
62	0	59	0	62	0	65	0
63	0	60	0	63	0	66	0
64	0	61	0	64	0	67	0
65	0	62	0	65	0	68	0
66	0	63	0	66	0	69	0
67	7	64	5	67	7	70	4
68	0	65	0	68	0	71	0
69	0	66	0	69	0	72	0
70	0	67	0	70	0	73	0
Total	7		5		7		4

Male Surviving Spouses		Female Surviving Spouses	
Attained age	Number	Attained age	Number
58	0	52	0
59	0	53	0
60	0	54	0
61	0	55	0
62	0	56	0
63	0	57	0
64	0	58	0
65	0	59	0
66	0	60	0
67	0	61	0
68	0	62	0
69	0	63	0
70	0	64	0
71	0	65	0
72	0	66	0
73	0	67	0
Total	0		0

Standard Assumptions

Following is a summary of those standard assumptions that apply to all groups. In some cases these assumptions differ from those in the Academy study.

Economic Assumptions

(1) General inflation: 3.5 percent
(2) Per capita growth in Gross National Product: 5 percent
(3) Discount rate/rate of investment return: 7 percent
(4) Salary increases: See table A.7 for sample percentages.

TABLE A.7
Percentage Increase in Salary for Continuing and New Employees

Age	Continuing Employee	New Employee
25	8.5%	5.0%
30	8.0	5.0
35	7.5	5.0
40	7.0	5.0
45	6.5	5.0
50	6.0	5.0
55	5.5	5.0
60	5.0	5.0

Mortality—1983 Group Annuity Mortality Table

Marital Status

Percentage Married at Retirement—Rates based on 1982 Social Security Old Age, Survivors, and Disability Insurance (OASDI) projections. See table A.8 for sample values.

TABLE A.8
Percentage of Employees Married at Retirement

Age at Retirement	Male Employee	Female Employee
55	81.1%	71.3%
56	81.0	70.4
57	80.8	69.6
58	80.6	68.7
59	80.3	66.8
60	80.0	65.7
61	79.8	64.5
62	79.6	63.3
63	79.3	61.9
64	79.0	60.3
65	78.8	58.5

Age Differences—A male is assumed to be three years older than his spouse.

Benefit Costs

Variation in per capita plan costs by age: 2.5 percent per year (table A.9).

TABLE A.9
Sample Average Annual Per Capita Costs by Age: First Year

Age	Retiree	Spouse
55	$781	$703
60	884	795
65	250	225
70	283	255
75	320	288
80	362	326

Group-Specific Assumptions

Following is a summary of those assumptions that vary by group. In some cases these assumptions differ from those in the Academy study.

Retirement Rates
The following rates of retirement are used:

TABLE A.10
Assumed Rates of Retirement

Age	Group A	Group F	Group H
55	3%	5%	3%
56	3	5	3
57	3	5	3
58	3	5	3
59	3	5	3
60	10	10	3
61	10	10	3
62	15	25	10
63	15	15	10
64	15	30	10
65	100	100	100

Disability and Separation

(1) Group A
   (a) *Disability*—1965–69 Society of Actuaries Inter-Company disability rates.
   (b) *Separation*—Select and ultimate rates. See table A.11 for sample values.

TABLE A.11
Sample Annual Separation Rates Per 100 Employees: Group A

Age at Employment	1	2	3	4	5 or more
25	29.04	27.04	24.04	21.04	13.92
35	19.36	17.36	14.36	11.36	6.04
45	13.80	11.80	8.80	5.80	1.80
55	10.40	8.40	5.40	2.40	—

Years of Service

(2) Group F
   (a) *Disability*—Graduated rates. See table A.12 for sample values.
   (b) *Separation*—Select and ultimate rates. See table A.12 for sample values.

TABLE A.12
Sample Annual Rates Per 100 Employees: Group F

	Attained Age	Disability	\multicolumn{5}{c}{Separation: Years of Service}

	Attained Age	Disability	1	2	3	4	5 or more
Males:	25	.090	26.34	21.84	20.46	18.48	16.50
	30	.090	24.14	20.94	19.36	17.16	14.90
	35	.090	22.34	20.24	18.26	15.18	13.20
	40	.138	22.00	19.80	17.60	14.30	11.60
	45	.314	21.12	19.50	17.60	14.30	9.90
	50	.524	18.74	17.98	16.96	14.08	7.20
	55	.933	10.56	9.60	6.84	3.64	—
	60	1.386	—	—	—	—	—
	65	—	—	—	—	—	—
Females:	25	.090	38.94	32.48	29.04	27.72	24.20
	30	.090	31.24	27.22	24.64	23.54	22.00
	35	.090	26.66	24.22	21.12	20.24	17.60
	40	.138	24.54	22.44	19.80	17.60	14.30
	45	.314	24.20	22.00	19.80	17.60	12.10
	50	.524	21.16	20.38	19.16	17.28	8.80
	55	.933	12.80	10.92	7.72	4.08	—
	60	1.386	—	—	—	—	—
	65	—	—	—	—	—	—

(3) Group H
   (a) *Disability*—Graduated rates. See table A.13 for sample values.
   (b) *Separation*—Select and ultimate rates. See table A.13 for sample values.

TABLE A.13
Sample Annual Rates Per 100 Employees: Group H

Attained Age	Disability	1	2	3	4	5 or more
20	.09	27.91	25.23	21.19	15.12	9.91
30	.11	21.72	18.54	13.85	8.37	6.78
40	.15	13.63	10.83	7.45	4.05	1.50
50	.33	9.43	7.42	5.06	2.42	.00
60	1.18	5.82	4.03	2.06	.08	.00
65	—	—	—	—	—	—

Growth Pattern

Each group was assigned one of the following growth rates based upon the history and forecast of the underlying company and industry.

(1) *Group A and Group H*—Increase of 2 percent per year in number of active employees. This results in approximately a 50 percent increase over a 20-year period.

(2) *Group F*—Two different assumptions were used:
   (a) Decrease of 2 percent per year in number of active employees. This results in approximately a one-third decrease in total number of employees over a 20-year period.
   (b) Decrease of 7 percent per year in number of active employees. This results in approximately a 50 percent decrease in total number of employees over a 10-year period.

New Entrants

Distributions of new entrants and their initial salaries were based on each group's distribution of initial active employees with 1.5 years of service. New entrants are assumed to have 1.5 years of service at plan entry and are equally divided between males and females at each age. See table A.14 for age distributions.

TABLE A.14
Assumed Age Distribution of New Entrants

Age at Entry	Group A	Group F	Group H
22	41.0%	36.0%	20.0%
27	21.6	29.6	28.4
32	12.6	11.2	14.0
37	8.6	7.2	10.6
42	6.0	4.0	9.6
47	2.6	5.6	7.0
52	4.6	4.8	5.2
57	2.4	1.6	4.4
62	0.6	0.0	0.8

Percentage of New Entrants

Appendix B
Funding Scenarios:
Illustrative Annual Values

The tables in appendix B present sample values generated under alternative retiree medical funding scenarios for each of the three model groups. These funding scenarios are based on 50-year open group projections, in which the number of employees and retirees for each group are projected by year, taking into account new employees hired in future years. Benefit payments and fund accumulations are then simulated for each year, using a range of advance funding methods and three different trend scenarios (high, medium, and low).

Description

Following is a description of the values included in each table.

(1) *Trend* is the annual rate of change in per capita plan costs due to factors other than changes in the group's composition by age or marital status.
   (a) *Expected trend* is the trend that is assumed, in the given year's actuarial valuation, to apply for all future years.
   (b) *Actual trend* is the trend that is actually experienced in the given year.
(2) *Normal cost* is the cost assigned by that funding method to the given plan year.
(3) *Amortization payment* is the annual amount payable to eliminate the unfunded liability over an appropriate period of time.
   (a) Under *maximum deductible* funding, amortization of the initial unfunded liability and any change in liability due to assumption changes (e.g., expected trend), is over a rolling 10-year period.
   (b) Under *minimum ERISA* funding, amortization of the initial unfunded liability, and any change in liability for assumption changes, occurs over 30 years.
(4) *Fund* is the current value of accumulated contributions, increased due to investment income and reduced due to actual payment of benefits.
(5) *Benefit payments* represent the actual payments of retiree medical benefits attributable to the given year; these payments are treated as reductions to the fund.
(6) *End-of-year contribution* is the actual cash contribution made to the fund at the end of the year under the given funding method. These

contributions are subject to "full funding limitations," which reduce the contribution that would otherwise be made, if the current fund accumulation exceeds current liabilities as defined for that funding method. In some instances the maximum deductible contribution is smaller than the minimum ERISA contribution for the same funding method due to the full funding limitations under current pension plan funding rules.

(7) *SFAS (Statement of Financial Accounting Standards) expense* is the annual expense that would be attributable to the given year if the Financial Accounting Standards Board's SFAS 87 standards were applied to these retiree medical benefits.

(8) *SFAS prepaid/(accrued) expense* represents the cumulative excess or deficiency of cash contributions over corresponding SFAS 87 expense amounts.

The tables are presented in the following order:
Group A
Group F—2% Rate of Decline
Group F—7% Rate of Decline
Group H

For each group, there is a low, medium, and high trend scenario; for each trend scenario, a range of funding scenarios are presented, distinguished by different funding methods.

TABLE B.1
Funding Scenarios: Illustrative Annual Values
Group A: Low Trend Scenario
(millions of dollars)

				Beginning of Year						Application of SFAS 87 Standards	
Funding Method	Year	Expected Trend	Actual Trend	Normal cost	Amortization payment	Fund	Benefit Payments	End-of-Year Contribution	Expense	Prepaid/ (accrued) expense[a]
Entry Age Normal, Maximum Deductible	0	—	—	$ 6	$13	$ 0	$ 2	$ 20	$ 13	$ 0
	5	9%	9%	9	6	104	3	15	10	38
	10	7	7	8	−4	181	4	0	6	38
	15	6	6	10	0	224	6	0	7	7
	20	5	5	11	0	267	9	0	5	−15
	25	5	5	16	0	351	14	17	12	−11
	30	5	5	22	1	501	21	25	18	20
	35	5	5	32	1	713	31	35	28	55
	40	5	5	45	2	1,010	44	50	40	99
	45	5	5	63	2	1,427	62	70	57	156
	50	5	5	89	3	2,012	88	99	81	232
Projected Unit Credit, Maximum Deductible	0	—	—	5	10	0	2	16	13	0
	5	9	9	7	5	81	3	13	12	12
	10	7	7	8	−3	150	4	0	8	3
	15	6	6	10	0	185	6	0	10	−39
	20	5	5	11	0	221	9	11	7	−70
	25	5	5	16	0	324	14	16	13	−50

(continued)

TABLE B.1 (continued)

Funding Method	Year	Expected Trend	Actual Trend	Normal cost	Amortization payment	Fund	Benefit Payments	End-of-Year Contribution	Expense	Prepaid/ (accrued) expense[a]
Project Unit Credit, Maximum Deductible (continued)	30	5%	5%	$ 22	$ 0	$ 466	$21	$ 23	$ 20	$ −34
	35	5	5	31	0	663	31	32	30	−21
	40	5	5	44	0	938	44	45	43	−10
	45	5	5	62	0	1,324	62	64	62	1
	50	5	5	87	0	1,865	88	90	87	12
Entry Age Normal, Minimum	0	—	—	6	7	0	2	14	14	0
	5	9	9	9	5	74	3	14	12	6
ERISA	10	7	7	8	−1	158	4	0	7	16
	15	6	6	10	0	213	6	0	8	−3
	20	5	5	11	0	252	9	3	6	−29
	25	5	5	16	0	350	14	17	12	−10
	30	5	5	22	1	500	21	25	19	19
	35	5	5	32	1	711	31	35	28	53
	40	5	5	45	2	1,006	44	50	40	96
	45	5	5	63	2	1,423	62	70	57	152
	50	5	5	89	3	2,007	88	99	81	227
Projected Unit Credit, Minimum	0	—	—	5	5	0	2	11	14	0
	5	9	9	7	4	58	3	12	13	−11
	10	7	7	8	0	130	4	4	9	−18
ERISA	15	6	6	10	0	184	6	0	10	−39

20	5	5	11		221	9	11	7	−69
25	5	5	16		324	14	16	13	−50
30	5	5	22	0	466	21	23	20	−34
35	5	5	31	0	663	31	32	30	−21
40	5	5	44	0	938	44	45	43	−10
45	5	5	62	0	1,324	62	64	62	1
50	5	5	87	0	1,865	88	90	87	12

				Beginning of Year				Application of SFAS 87 Standards	
Funding Method	Year	Expected Trend	Actual Trend	Normal cost	Fund	Benefit Payments	End-of-Year Contribution	Expense	Prepaid/ (accrued) expense[a]
Aggregate	0	—	—	$14	$ 0	$ 2	$15	$14	$ 0
	5	9%	9%	13	78	3	14	12	10
	10	7	7	6	159	4	0	7	16
	15	6	6	7	212	6	0	8	−5
	20	5	5	9	250	9	5	6	−32
	25	5	5	15	342	14	16	12	−18
	30	5	5	22	479	21	23	20	−2
	35	5	5	31	673	31	34	30	14
	40	5	5	45	944	44	48	45	32
	45	5	5	64	1,325	62	68	64	53
	50	5	5	90	1,862	88	97	91	80

(continued)

TABLE B.1 (continued)

Funding Method	Year	Expected Trend	Actual Trend	Normal cost	Amortization payment	Fund	Benefit Payments	End-of-Year Contribution
Unprojected Unit Credit, Maximum Deductible	0	—	—	$1	$2	$0	$2	$3
	5	0%	9%	1	3	8	3	5
	10	0	7	2	3	27	4	5
	15	0	6	3	3	46	6	7
	20	0	5	5	5	70	9	10
	25	0	5	7	7	103	14	15
	30	0	5	9	12	150	21	23
	35	0	5	13	18	222	31	33
	40	0	5	18	26	327	44	47
	45	0	5	26	36	477	62	66
	50	0	5	36	50	690	88	92
Unprojected Unit Credit, Minimum ERISA	0	—	—	1	1	0	2	2
	5	0	9	1	2	2	3	3
	10	0	7	2	3	10	4	6
	15	0	6	3	5	28	6	9
	20	0	5	5	6	53	9	11
	25	0	5	7	8	85	14	16
	30	0	5	9	11	130	21	22
	35	0	5	13	17	191	31	33
	40	0	5	18	25	281	44	47
	45	0	5	26	36	412	62	66
	50	0	5	36	50	599	88	92

[a]Prepaid/(accrued) expense is the cumulative excess/(deficiency) of cash contributions over annual SFAS 87 expense amounts.

TABLE B.2
Funding Scenarios: Illustrative Annual Values
Group A: Medium Trend Scenario
(millions of dollars)

				Beginning of Year						Application of SFAS 87 Standards	
Funding Method	Year	Expected Trend	Actual Trend	Normal cost	Amortization payment	Fund	Benefit Payments	End-of-Year Contribution		Expense	Prepaid/ (accrued) expense[a]
Entry Age Normal, Maximum Deductible	0	—	—	$ 6	$13	$ 0	$ 2	$20		$13	$ 0
	5	10%	10%	12	13	115	3	27		14	44
	10	9	9	15	1	235	4	18		14	68
	15	8	8	19	0	322	7	20		16	29
	20	7	7	23	0	426	12	24		15	−6
	25	6	6	26	0	544	19	28		17	−31
	30	5	5	30	0	668	28	32		19	−59
	35	5	5	42	1	944	41	46		33	6
	40	5	5	60	2	1,334	58	66		50	78
	45	5	5	84	3	1,885	83	93		73	164
	50	5	5	118	4	2,658	117	131		106	272
Projected Unit Credit, Maximum Deductible	0	—	—	5	10	0	2	16		13	0
	5	10	10	10	10	88	3	21		16	15
	10	9	9	13	1	188	4	16		17	15
	15	8	8	17	0	274	7	19		19	−26
	20	7	7	21	0	375	12	23		18	−67
	25	6	6	25	0	492	19	27		20	−98

(continued)

TABLE B.2 (continued)

Funding Method	Year	Expected Trend	Actual Trend	Normal cost	Beginning of Year Amortization payment	Fund	Benefit Payments	End-of-Year Contribution	Expense	Prepaid/(accrued) expense[a]
Projected Unit Credit, Maximum Deductible (continued)	30	5%	5%	$ 29	$ 0	$ 617	$ 28	$ 30	$ 22	$ -132
	35	5	5	41	0	878	41	42	36	-93
	40	5	5	58	0	1,243	58	60	54	-62
	45	5	5	82	0	1,753	83	84	79	-36
	50	5	5	115	-1	2,470	117	119	114	-12
Entry Age Normal, Minimum	0	—	—	6	7	0	2	14	14	0
	5	10	10	12	7	80	3	21	17	8
	10	9	9	15	4	192	4	21	17	23
ERISA	15	8	8	19	0	322	7	20	16	31
	20	7	7	23	0	426	12	24	15	-4
	25	6	6	26	0	544	19	28	17	-30
	30	5	5	30	0	668	28	32	19	-58
	35	5	5	42	1	943	41	46	33	6
	40	5	5	60	2	1,331	58	66	50	75
	45	5	5	84	3	1,879	83	93	74	158
	50	5	5	118	4	2,649	117	131	106	263
Projected Unit Credit, Minimum	0	—	—	5	5	0	2	11	14	0
	5	10	10	10	6	62	3	16	18	-12
	10	9	9	13	3	154	4	18	19	-19
ERISA	15	8	8	17	0	274	7	19	19	-24
	20	7	7	21	0	375	12	23	18	-65
	25	6	6	25	0	492	19	27	20	-97

30	5	5	29	0	617	28	30	22	−131
35	5	5	41	0	878	41	42	36	−93
40	5	5	58	0	1,243	58	60	54	−62
45	5	5	82	0	1,753	83	84	79	−36
50	5	5	115	0	2,470	117	119	114	−12

				Beginning of Year				Application of SFAS 87 Standards	
Funding Method	Year	Expected Trend	Actual Trend	Normal cost	Fund	Benefit Payments	End-of-Year Contribution	Expense	Prepaid/ (accrued) expense[a]
Aggregate	0	—	—	$14	$ 0	$ 2	$15	$14	$ 0
	5	10%	10%	19	84	3	20	17	12
	10	9	9	18	193	4	19	16	25
	15	8	8	18	318	7	19	17	27
	20	7	7	21	426	12	22	15	−4
	25	6	6	23	544	19	25	17	−30
	30	5	5	25	667	28	27	20	−58
	35	5	5	39	918	41	42	35	−20
	40	5	5	57	1,273	58	61	55	15
	45	5	5	83	1,775	83	88	81	51
	50	5	5	118	2,482	117	126	118	93

(continued)

TABLE B.2 (continued)

Funding Method	Year	Expected Trend	Actual Trend	Normal cost	Beginning of Year Amortization payment	Fund	Benefit Payments	End-of-Year Contribution
Unprojected Unit Credit, Maximum Deductible	0	—	—	$1	$2	$0	$2	$3
	5	0%	10%	1	3	8	3	5
	10	0	9	2	3	27	4	6
	15	0	8	4	5	49	7	9
	20	0	7	6	7	81	12	14
	25	0	6	9	11	128	19	21
	30	0	5	12	17	196	28	31
	35	0	5	17	24	294	41	44
	40	0	5	24	34	433	58	62
	45	0	5	34	47	632	83	87
	50	0	5	48	66	914	117	122
Unprojected Unit Credit, Minimum ERISA	0	—	—	1	1	0	2	2
	5	0	10	1	2	2	3	4
	10	0	9	2	4	11	4	6
	15	0	8	4	6	30	7	10
	20	0	7	6	8	60	12	15
	25	0	6	9	12	104	19	22
	30	0	5	12	16	167	28	31
	35	0	5	17	24	251	41	44
	40	0	5	24	34	372	58	62
	45	0	5	34	47	546	83	87
	50	0	5	48	66	794	117	122

Unit Credit with No Trend or Discount Rate, Maximum Deductible	0	—	—	2	6	0	2	9
	5	0	10	4	7	44	3	12
	10	0	9	8	5	118	4	14
	15	0	8	14	2	222	7	17
	20	0	7	21	0	375	12	23
	25	0	6	32	−1	577	19	28
	30	0	5	44	−2	832	28	30
	35	0	5	63	−3	1,182	41	43
	40	0	5	88	−4	1,670	58	60
	45	0	5	125	−6	2,355	83	85
	50	0	5	176	−9	3,317	117	120
Projected Unit Credit with 5% Cap on Trend, Maximum Deductible	0	—	—	1	4	0	2	6
	5	5	10	3	5	29	3	9
	10	5	9	5	5	78	4	11
	15	5	8	9	4	151	7	14
	20	5	7	14	5	256	12	20
	25	5	6	21	5	409	19	27
	30	5	5	29	1	615	28	32
	35	5	5	41	0	878	41	42
	40	5	5	58	0	1,243	58	60
	45	5	5	82	0	1,753	83	84
	50	5	5	115	−1	2,470	117	119

(continued)

TABLE B.2 (continued)

Funding Method	Year	Expected Trend	Actual Trend	Normal cost	Amortization payment	Fund	Benefit Payments	End-of-Year Contribution
Unit Credit with No Trend or Discount Rate, Minimum ERISA	0	—	—	$ 2	$ 3	$ 0	$ 2	$ 6
	5	0%	10%	4	4	28	3	9
	10	0	9	8	5	83	4	14
	15	0	8	14	6	182	7	21
	20	0	7	21	6	342	12	29
	25	0	6	32	0	572	19	33
	30	0	5	44	−2	833	28	30
	35	0	5	63	−2	1,183	41	43
	40	0	5	88	−3	1,671	58	60
	45	0	5	125	−5	2,356	83	85
	50	0	5	176	−7	3,319	117	120
Projected Unit Credit with 5% Cap on Trend, Minimum ERISA	0	—	—	1	2	0	2	4
	5	5	10	3	3	17	3	7
	10	5	9	5	5	52	4	11
	15	5	8	9	6	117	7	16
	20	5	7	14	8	224	12	24
	25	5	6	21	8	385	19	31
	30	5	5	29	4	604	28	36
	35	5	5	41	0	879	41	42
	40	5	5	58	0	1,243	58	60
	45	5	5	82	0	1,753	83	84
	50	5	5	115	0	2,470	117	119

[a]Prepaid/(accrued) expense is the cumulative excess/(deficiency) of cash contributions over annual SFAS 87 expense amounts.

TABLE B.3
Funding Scenarios: Illustrative Annual Values
Group A: High Trend Scenario
(millions of dollars)

				Beginning of Year					End-of-Year Contribution	Application of SFAS 87 Standards	
Funding Method	Year	Expected Trend	Actual Trend	Normal cost	Amortization payment	Fund	Benefit Payments			Expense	Prepaid/(accrued) expense[a]
Entry Age Normal, Maximum Deductible	0	—	—	$6	$13	$0	$2		$20	$13	$0
	5	10%	10%	12	13	115	3		27	14	44
	10	9	9	16	0	244	4		14	13	63
	15	8	8	20	−11	423	8		0	11	82
	20	8	8	33	0	568	13		35	22	39
	25	7	7	40	0	787	22		6	26	20
	30	6	6	47	0	1,117	35		0	22	40
	35	6	6	70	1	1,457	54		76	51	14
	40	5	5	79	0	1,777	77		85	55	−81
	45	5	5	111	2	2,497	109		122	89	72
	50	5	5	157	5	3,515	155		173	134	245
Projected Unit Credit, Maximum Deductible	0	—	—	5	10	0	2		16	13	0
	5	10	10	10	10	88	3		21	16	15
	10	9	9	14	0	196	4		15	16	10
	15	8	8	18	−8	350	8		0	15	1
	20	8	8	30	0	490	13		32	27	−51
	25	7	7	37	0	681	22		27	31	−105

(continued)

TABLE B.3 (continued)

Funding Method	Year	Expected Trend	Actual Trend	Normal cost	Amortization payment	Fund	Benefit Payments	End-of-Year Contribution	Expense	Prepaid/ (accrued) expense[a]
Projected Unit Credit, Maximum Deductible (continued)	30	6%	6%	$ 45	$ 0	$ 998	$ 35	$ 0	$ 29	$ −106
	35	6	6	67	0	1,331	54	70	58	−153
	40	5	5	77	0	1,646	77	79	61	−271
	45	5	5	108	0	2,322	109	112	97	−189
	50	5	5	152	−1	3,271	155	158	145	−122
Entry Age Normal, Minimum ERISA	0	—	—	6	7	0	2	14	14	0
	5	10	10	12	7	80	3	21	17	8
	10	9	9	16	3	208	4	20	15	28
	15	8	8	20	−4	396	8	0	13	56
	20	8	8	33	0	568	13	35	22	42
	25	7	7	40	0	787	22	6	26	22
	30	6	6	47	0	1,116	35	0	22	41
	35	6	6	70	0	1,457	54	76	51	15
	40	5	5	79	0	1,777	77	85	55	−80
	45	5	5	111	2	2,496	109	121	89	71
	50	5	5	157	4	3,509	155	172	135	239
Projected Unit Credit, Minimum ERISA	0	—	—	5	5	0	2	11	14	0
	5	10	10	10	6	62	3	16	18	−12
	10	9	9	14	2	166	4	17	18	−20
	15	8	8	18	−3	324	8	0	17	−25
	20	8	8	30	0	490	13	32	27	−49
	25	7	7	37	0	681	22	27	31	−103

Year	Expected Trend	Actual Trend	Normal cost	Fund		Benefit Payments	End-of-Year Contribution	Expense	Prepaid/(accrued) expense
30	6	6	45	998	0	35	0	29	−104
35	6	6	67	1,331	0	54	70	58	−152
40	5	5	77	1,646	0	77	79	61	−270
45	5	5	108	2,322	0	109	112	97	−189
50	5	5	152	3,271	−1	155	158	145	−122

				Beginning of Year				Application of SFAS 87 Standards	
Funding Method	Year	Expected Trend	Actual Trend	Normal cost	Fund	Benefit Payments	End-of-Year Contribution	Expense	Prepaid/ (accrued) expense[a]
Aggregate	0	—	—	$14	$ 0	$ 2	$ 15	$14	$ 0
	5	10%	10%	19	84	3	20	17	12
	10	9	9	17	210	4	18	15	29
	15	8	8	14	390	8	0	13	50
	20	8	8	31	564	13	33	23	37
	25	7	7	34	776	22	18	26	11
	30	6	6	30	1,103	35	0	23	28
	35	6	6	63	1,442	54	68	53	−1
	40	5	5	67	1,777	77	72	56	−79
	45	5	5	102	2,427	109	109	95	0
	50	5	5	150	3,352	155	161	146	77

(continued)

TABLE B.3 (continued)

Funding Method	Year	Expected Trend	Actual Trend	Normal cost	Amortization payment	Fund	Benefit Payments	End-of-Year Contribution
Unprojected Unit Credit, Maximum Deductible	0	—	—	$1	$2	$0	$2	$3
	5	0%	10%	1	3	8	3	5
	10	0	9	2	3	27	4	6
	15	0	8	4	5	50	8	10
	20	0	8	6	9	86	13	16
	25	0	7	10	15	142	22	27
	30	0	6	15	24	231	35	42
	35	0	6	23	36	367	54	62
	40	0	5	32	47	563	77	85
	45	0	5	45	62	833	109	115
	50	0	5	64	87	1,203	155	161
Unprojected Unit Credit, Minimum ERISA	0	—	—	1	1	0	2	2
	5	0	10	1	2	2	3	4
	10	0	9	2	4	11	4	6
	15	0	8	4	6	31	8	11
	20	0	8	6	9	64	13	17
	25	0	7	10	15	115	22	27
	30	0	6	15	23	192	35	41
	35	0	6	23	34	306	54	61
	40	0	5	32	48	475	77	85
	45	0	5	45	64	713	109	117
	50	0	5	64	87	1,044	155	162

[a]Prepaid/(accrued) expense is the cumulative excess/(deficiency) of cash contributions over annual SFAS 87 expense amounts.

TABLE B.4
Funding Scenarios: Illustrative Annual Values
Group F—2% Rate of Decline: Low Trend Scenario
(millions of dollars)

				Beginning of Year					Application of SFAS 87 Standards	
Funding Method	Year	Expected Trend	Actual Trend	Normal cost	Amortization payment	Fund	Benefit Payments	End-of-Year Contribution	Expense	Prepaid/ (accrued) expense[a]
Entry Age Normal, Maximum Deductible	0	—	—	$3	$17	$0	$3	$21	$17	$0
	5	9%	9%	4	10	92	5	15	12	24
	10	7	7	4	-2	156	6	0	6	25
	15	6	6	4	0	175	9	0	-1	-5
	20	5	5	4	0	189	11	0	-1	8
	25	5	5	4	0	197	13	0	1	10
	30	5	5	5	0	200	14	5	4	0
	35	5	5	6	0	225	16	6	5	8
	40	5	5	7	0	256	18	7	6	15
	45	5	5	8	0	292	20	8	7	20
	50	5	5	9	0	335	22	10	9	25
Projected Unit Credit, Maximum Deductible	0	—	—	4	14	0	3	19	17	0
	5	9	9	4	9	81	5	14	12	11
	10	7	7	4	-2	140	6	0	7	7
	15	6	6	4	0	154	9	0	0	-28
	20	5	5	4	0	160	11	0	0	-23
	25	5	5	5	0	168	13	5	3	-21

(continued)

TABLE B.4 (continued)

Funding Method	Year	Expected Trend	Actual Trend	Normal cost	Beginning of Year Amortization payment	Fund	Benefit Payments	End-of-Year Contribution	Expense	Prepaid/(accrued) expense[a]
Projected Unit Credit, Maximum Deductible (continued)	30	5%	5%	$5	$0	$189	$14	$6	$4	$−12
	35	5	5	6	0	212	16	7	6	−6
	40	5	5	7	0	240	18	8	7	−2
	45	5	5	8	0	274	20	9	8	0
	50	5	5	10	0	315	22	10	10	2
Entry Age Normal, Minimum ERISA	0	—	—	3	9	0	3	13	17	0
	5	9	9	4	7	52	5	12	14	−18
	10	7	7	4	3	102	6	7	9	−30
	15	6	6	4	1	139	9	6	1	−40
	20	5	5	4	0	157	11	4	1	−23
	25	5	5	4	0	178	13	5	3	−8
	30	5	5	5	0	200	14	6	4	3
	35	5	5	6	0	225	16	6	5	10
	40	5	5	7	0	255	18	7	6	16
	45	5	5	8	0	292	20	9	7	21
	50	5	5	9	0	335	22	10	9	26
Projected Unit Credit, Minimum ERISA	0	—	—	4	8	0	3	12	17	0
	5	9	9	4	6	48	5	11	15	−23
	10	7	7	4	3	94	6	7	10	−39
	15	6	6	4	1	129	9	6	2	−52
	20	5	5	4	0	149	11	4	1	−33
	25	5	5	5	0	168	13	5	3	−19

	30	5	5	5	0	189	14	6	4	−10
	35	5	5	6	0	212	16	7	6	−5
	40	5	5	7	0	240	18	8	7	−2
	45	5	5	8	0	274	20	9	8	1
	50	5	5	10	0	315	22	10	10	3

				Beginning of Year				Application of SFAS 87 Standards	
Funding Method	Year	Expected Trend	Actual Trend	Normal cost	Fund	Benefit Payments	End-of-Year Contribution	Expense	Prepaid/ (accrued) expense[a]
Aggregate	0	—	—	$20	$0	$3	$22	$17	$0
	5	9%	9%	12	87	5	13	12	18
	10	7	7	3	145	6	0	7	14
	15	6	6	2	168	9	0	0	−12
	20	5	5	0	179	11	0	−1	−2
	25	5	5	3	183	13	0	2	−5
	30	5	5	5	199	14	5	4	0
	35	5	5	6	222	16	6	5	6
	40	5	5	7	251	18	7	6	11
	45	5	5	8	286	20	8	8	15
	50	5	5	9	328	22	10	9	19

(continued)

TABLE B.4 (continued)

Funding Method	Year	Expected Trend	Actual Trend	Normal cost	Beginning of Year Amortization payment	Fund	Benefit Payments	End-of-Year Contribution
Unprojected Unit Credit, Maximum Deductible	0	—	—	$1	$4	$ 0	$3	$ 5
	5	0%	9%	1	7	13	5	8
	10	0	7	1	6	42	6	8
	15	0	6	2	6	63	9	9
	20	0	5	2	6	82	11	9
	25	0	5	2	7	101	13	10
	30	0	5	3	7	121	14	11
	35	0	5	3	8	147	16	12
	40	0	5	3	9	181	18	13
	45	0	5	4	10	226	20	15
	50	0	5	5	12	285	22	17
Unprojected Unit Credit, Minimum ERISA	0	—	—	1	2	0	3	3
	5	0	9	1	5	0	5	6
	10	0	7	1	7	7	6	9
	15	0	6	2	9	25	9	12
	20	0	5	2	10	49	11	13
	25	0	5	2	10	75	13	13
	30	0	5	3	8	105	14	12
	35	0	5	3	9	129	16	13
	40	0	5	3	10	161	18	14
	45	0	5	4	11	203	20	16
	50	0	5	5	13	260	22	19

[a]Prepaid/(accrued) expense is the cumulative excess/(deficiency) of cash contributions over annual SFAS 87 expense amounts.

TABLE B.5
Funding Scenarios: Illustrative Annual Values
Group F—2% Rate of Decline: Medium Trend Scenario
(millions of dollars)

					Beginning of Year				Application of SFAS 87 Standards	
Funding Method	Year	Expected Trend	Actual Trend	Normal cost	Amortization payment	Fund	Benefit Payments	End-of-Year Contribution	Expense	Prepaid/ (accrued) expense[a]
Entry Age Normal, Maximum Deductible	0	—	—	$3	$17	$0	$3	$21	$17	$0
	5	10%	10%	5	16	100	5	23	15	28
	10	9	9	6	6	189	7	13	12	39
	15	8	8	7	0	234	10	0	4	7
	20	7	7	7	0	261	13	0	3	0
	25	6	6	7	0	278	17	0	2	−3
	30	5	5	7	0	285	19	0	2	−3
	35	5	5	8	0	298	21	8	5	−5
	40	5	5	9	0	338	23	10	7	9
	45	5	5	10	0	387	26	11	9	21
	50	5	5	12	0	443	30	13	11	29
Projected Unit Credit, Maximum Deductible	0	—	—	4	14	0	3	19	17	0
	5	10	10	5	14	88	5	21	16	14
	10	9	9	7	5	167	7	13	13	16
	15	8	8	7	0	207	10	8	5	−22
	20	7	7	7	0	234	13	5	5	−28
	25	6	6	7	0	248	17	5	4	−35

(continued)

125

TABLE B.5 (continued)

Funding Method	Year	Expected Trend	Actual Trend	Normal cost	Amortization payment	Fund	Benefit Payments	End-of-Year Contribution	Expense	Prepaid/(accrued) expense[a]
Projected Unit Credit, Maximum Deductible (continued)	30	5%	5%	$7	$0	$252	$19	$5	$3	$−38
	35	5	5	8	0	281	21	9	6	−24
	40	5	5	10	0	318	23	10	8	−13
	45	5	5	11	0	363	26	12	11	−5
	50	5	5	13	0	417	30	14	13	−1
Entry Age Normal, Minimum ERISA	0	—	—	3	9	0	3	13	17	0
	5	10	10	5	9	56	5	16	19	−19
	10	9	9	6	7	120	7	14	16	−31
	15	8	8	7	4	186	10	12	7	−40
	20	7	7	7	1	243	13	9	4	−14
	25	6	6	7	0	265	17	6	3	−14
	30	5	5	7	0	274	19	0	3	−12
	35	5	5	8	0	298	21	8	5	−3
	40	5	5	9	0	338	23	10	7	10
	45	5	5	10	0	386	26	11	9	21
	50	5	5	12	0	444	30	13	11	30
Projected Unit Credit, Minimum ERISA	0	—	—	4	8	0	3	12	17	0
	5	10	10	5	8	51	5	14	19	−25
	10	9	9	7	6	109	7	13	17	−43
	15	8	8	7	3	170	10	11	8	−58
	20	7	7	7	1	222	13	9	5	−38
	25	6	6	7	0	246	17	8	4	−34

Year								
30	5	5	7	0	252	19	5	4	−36
35	5	5	8	0	281	21	9	6	−22
40	5	5	10	0	318	23	10	9	−12
45	5	5	11	0	363	26	12	11	−5
50	5	5	13	0	417	30	14	13	0

				Beginning of Year				Application of SFAS 87 Standards	
Funding Method	Year	Expected Trend	Actual Trend	Normal cost	Fund	Benefit Payments	End-of-Year Contribution	Expense	Prepaid/ (accrued) expense[a]
Aggregate	0	—	—	$20	$0	$3	$22	$17	$0
	5	10%	10%	17	92	5	18	16	19
	10	9	9	11	169	7	11	13	19
	15	8	8	7	227	10	7	4	0
	20	7	7	5	261	13	0	3	1
	25	6	6	4	278	17	0	3	−3
	30	5	5	3	285	19	0	2	−3
	35	5	5	7	297	21	8	5	−5
	40	5	5	9	335	23	9	8	6
	45	5	5	10	380	26	11	10	15
	50	5	5	12	435	30	13	12	22

(continued)

TABLE B.5 (continued)

Funding Method	Year	Expected Trend	Actual Trend	Normal cost	Beginning of Year Amortization payment	Fund	Benefit Payments	End-of-Year Contribution
				$1	$4	$0	$3	$5
Unprojected Unit Credit, Maximum Deductible	0	—	—					
	5	0%	10%	1	7	13	5	9
	10	0	9	1	6	43	7	8
	15	0	8	2	8	66	10	11
	20	0	7	2	10	94	13	13
	25	0	6	3	11	124	17	15
	30	0	5	3	11	157	19	15
	35	0	5	4	11	193	21	16
	40	0	5	5	12	237	23	18
	45	0	5	5	14	295	26	20
	50	0	5	6	16	372	30	23
Unprojected Unit Credit, Minimum ERISA	0	—	—					
	5	0	10	1	2	0	3	3
	10	0	9	1	5	0	5	6
	15	0	8	1	7	8	7	9
	20	0	7	2	11	27	10	14
	25	0	6	2	13	56	13	16
		0		3	14	90	17	18
	30	0	5	3	12	131	19	17
	35	0	5	4	13	167	21	18
	40	0	5	5	13	210	23	19
	45	0	5	5	15	265	26	22
	50	0	5	6	17	339	30	25

Unit Credit with	0	—	—	2	9	0	3	12
No Trend or	5	0	10	3	10	48	5	14
Discount Rate,	10	0	9	4	7	115	7	12
Maximum	15	0	8	6	2	176	10	9
Deductible	20	0	7	7	0	232	13	7
	25	0	6	9	0	275	17	7
	30	0	5	10	−1	311	19	5
	35	0	5	12	−1	350	21	6
	40	0	5	14	−1	397	23	7
	45	0	5	16	−1	454	26	8
	50	0	5	18	−1	522	30	9
Projected Unit	0	—	—	1	7	0	3	9
Credit with 5%	5	5	10	2	9	33	5	11
Cap on Trend,	10	5	9	3	8	80	7	11
Maximum	15	5	8	4	5	127	10	10
Deductible	20	5	7	5	4	170	13	10
	25	5	6	6	3	211	17	10
	30	5	5	7	−2	252	19	4
	35	5	5	8	0	279	21	9
	40	5	5	10	0	316	23	10
	45	5	5	11	0	360	26	12
	50	5	5	13	0	412	30	13

(continued)

TABLE B.5 (continued)

Funding Method	Year	Expected Trend	Actual Trend	Normal cost	Amortization payment	Fund	Benefit Payments	End-of-Year Contribution
Unit Credit with No Trend or Discount Rate, Minimum ERISA	0	—	—	$ 2	$ 5	$ 0	$ 3	$ 7
	5	0%	10%	3	6	24	5	10
	10	0	9	4	7	60	7	12
	15	0	8	6	8	114	10	15
	20	0	7	7	8	183	13	17
	25	0	6	9	3	258	17	13
	30	0	5	10	−1	311	19	5
	35	0	5	12	−1	350	21	6
	40	0	5	14	−1	398	23	7
	45	0	5	16	−1	454	26	8
	50	0	5	18	−1	522	30	9
Projected Unit Credit with 5% Cap on Trend, Minimum ERISA	0	—	—	1	4	0	3	6
	5	5	10	2	5	13	5	8
	10	5	9	3	7	36	7	11
	15	5	8	4	9	73	10	14
	20	5	7	5	10	123	13	16
	25	5	6	6	9	182	17	17
	30	5	5	7	5	250	19	13
	35	5	5	8	0	279	21	9
	40	5	5	10	0	315	23	10
	45	5	5	11	0	359	26	12
	50	5	5	13	0	411	30	13

[a]Prepaid/(accrued) expense is the cumulative excess/(deficiency) of cash contributions over annual SFAS 87 expense amounts.

TABLE B.6
Funding Scenarios: Illustrative Annual Values
Group F—2% Rate of Decline: High Trend Scenario
(millions of dollars)

Funding Method	Year	Expected Trend	Actual Trend	Normal cost	Amortization payment	Fund	Benefit Payments	End-of-Year Contribution	Expense	Prepaid/ (accrued) expense[a]
Entry Age Normal, Maximum Deductible	0	—	—	$ 3	$ 17	$ 0	$ 3	$ 21	$17	$ 0
	5	10%	10%	5	16	100	5	23	15	28
	10	9	9	6	0	202	7	7	11	44
	15	8	8	7	−5	280	10	0	0	23
	20	8	8	10	0	320	15	5	6	10
	25	7	7	10	0	369	19	0	4	9
	30	6	6	10	0	414	24	0	2	7
	35	6	6	12	0	441	28	13	8	−4
	40	5	5	12	0	462	31	0	6	−9
	45	5	5	13	0	511	35	15	10	4
	50	5	5	16	0	586	39	17	14	24
Projected Unit Credit, Maximum Deductible	0	—	—	4	14	0	3	19	17	0
	5	10	10	5	14	88	5	21	16	14
	10	9	9	7	0	180	7	7	12	20
	15	8	8	8	−4	251	10	0	2	−7
	20	8	8	10	0	287	15	11	8	−24
	25	7	7	10	0	332	19	0	7	−29

(continued)

TABLE B.6 (continued)

Funding Method	Year	Expected Trend	Actual Trend	Normal cost	Amortization payment	Fund	Benefit Payments	End-of-Year Contribution	Expense	Prepaid/(accrued) expense[a]
Projected Unit Credit, Maximum Deductible (continued)	30	6%	6%	$11	$0	$381	$24	$ 0	$ 4	$ −29
	35	6	6	13	0	410	28	14	10	−37
	40	5	5	13	0	423	31	12	8	−51
	45	5	5	15	0	481	35	16	12	−30
	50	5	5	17	0	552	39	18	16	−15
Entry Age Normal, Minimum ERISA	0	—	—	3	9	0	3	13	17	0
	5	10	10	5	9	56	5	16	19	−19
	10	9	9	6	6	129	7	14	15	−31
	15	8	8	7	2	217	10	10	4	−39
	20	8	8	10	2	295	15	13	8	−11
	25	7	7	10	0	348	19	9	5	−9
	30	6	6	10	0	414	24	0	2	10
	35	6	6	12	0	441	28	13	8	−3
	40	5	5	12	0	462	31	0	6	−8
	45	5	5	13	0	511	35	15	10	5
	50	5	5	16	0	586	39	17	14	24
Projected Unit Credit, Minimum ERISA	0	—	—	4	8	0	3	12	17	0
	5	10	10	5	8	51	5	14	19	−25
	10	9	9	7	5	117	7	13	16	−45
	15	8	8	8	2	195	10	10	6	−62
	20	8	8	10	2	267	15	13	9	−41
	25	7	7	10	0	320	19	11	7	−39

Year	Expected Trend	Actual Trend	Normal cost	Fund	Benefit Payments	End-of-Year Contribution	Expense	Prepaid/(accrued) expense
30	6	6	11	0	381	24	0	4	−26
35	6	6	13	0	410	28	14	10	−35
40	5	5	13	0	423	31	12	8	−50
45	5	5	15	0	481	35	16	12	−29
50	5	5	17	0	552	39	18	16	−14

				Beginning of Year			Application of SFAS 87 Standards	
Funding Method	Year	Expected Trend	Actual Trend	Normal cost	Fund	Benefit Payments	End-of-Year Contribution	Expense	Prepaid/(accrued) expense[a]
Aggregate	0	—	—	$ 20	$ 0	$ 3	$ 22	$ 17	$ 0
	5	10%	10%	17	92	5	18	16	19
	10	9	9	10	180	7	10	12	21
	15	8	8	3	266	10	0	1	10
	20	8	8	10	314	15	10	6	6
	25	7	7	7	368	19	0	4	10
	30	6	6	4	414	24	0	2	7
	35	6	6	12	441	28	12	8	−4
	40	5	5	9	461	31	0	6	−10
	45	5	5	13	508	35	14	10	1
	50	5	5	16	580	39	17	14	17

(continued)

TABLE B.6 (continued)

Funding Method	Year	Expected Trend	Actual Trend	Normal cost	Amortization payment	Fund	Benefit Payments	End-of-Year Contribution
Unprojected Unit Credit, Maximum Deductible	0	—	—	$1	$4	$0	$3	$5
	5	0%	10%	1	7	13	5	9
	10	0	9	1	7	43	7	9
	15	0	8	2	9	68	10	12
	20	0	8	3	12	99	15	15
	25	0	7	3	14	137	19	19
	30	0	6	4	16	182	24	22
	35	0	6	5	17	235	28	24
	40	0	5	6	17	299	31	25
	45	0	5	7	18	377	35	27
	50	0	5	8	21	473	39	31
Unprojected Unit Credit, Minimum ERISA	0	—	—	1	2	0	3	3
	5	0	10	1	5	0	5	6
	10	0	9	1	8	8	7	10
	15	0	8	2	11	28	10	14
	20	0	8	3	14	59	15	18
	25	0	7	3	17	97	19	22
	30	0	6	4	17	147	24	23
	35	0	6	5	19	197	28	26
	40	0	5	6	20	258	31	28
	45	0	5	7	21	334	35	30
	50	0	5	8	22	429	39	33

[a] Prepaid/(accrued) expense is the cumulative excess/(deficiency) of cash contributions over annual SFAS 87 expense amounts.

TABLE B.7
Funding Scenarios: Illustrative Annual Values
Group F—7% Rate of Decline: Low Trend Scenario
(millions of dollars)

Funding Method	Year	Expected Trend	Actual Trend	Normal cost	Amortization payment	Fund	Benefit Payments	End-of-Year Contribution	Expense	Prepaid/ (accrued) expense[a]
Entry Age Normal,										
Maximum	0	—	—	$3	$17	$0	$3	$21	$17	$0
Deductible	5	9%	9%	3	10	90	5	14	11	22
	10	7	7	2	−2	145	6	0	5	21
	15	6	6	2	0	161	8	0	−3	−2
	20	5	5	1	0	172	10	0	−4	21
	25	5	5	1	0	182	11	0	−4	43
	30	5	5	1	0	192	11	0	−5	66
	35	5	5	1	0	206	10	0	−7	93
	40	5	5	1	0	230	10	0	−9	130
	45	5	5	1	0	268	9	0	−12	181
	50	5	5	1	0	327	8	0	−17	251
Projected Unit										
Credit,	0	—	—	4	14	0	3	19	17	0
Maximum	5	9	9	4	9	79	5	13	12	11
Deductible	10	7	7	3	−2	131	6	0	6	7
	15	6	6	2	0	142	8	0	−2	−21
	20	5	5	2	0	145	10	0	−3	−6
	25	5	5	2	0	144	11	0	−2	5

(continued)

TABLE B.7 (continued)

Funding Method	Year	Expected Trend	Actual Trend	Normal cost	Amortization payment	Fund	Benefit Payments	End-of-Year Contribution	Expense	Prepaid/(accrued) expense[a]
Projected Unit Credit, Maximum Deductible (continued)	30	5%	5%	$1	$0	$138	$11	$0	$ −1	$ 13
	35	5	5	1	0	131	10	0	−1	19
	40	5	5	1	0	125	10	0	−1	26
	45	5	5	1	0	121	9	0	−2	34
	50	5	5	1	0	121	8	0	−3	45
Entry Age Normal, Minimum ERISA	0	—	—	3	9	0	3	13	17	0
	5	9	9	3	7	50	5	11	14	−20
	10	7	7	2	4	90	6	6	8	−34
	15	6	6	2	2	114	8	4	0	−48
	20	5	5	1	1	122	10	2	−1	−29
	25	5	5	1	1	123	11	2	0	−15
	30	5	5	1	0	118	11	1	0	−7
	35	5	5	1	0	108	10	1	0	−3
	40	5	5	1	0	97	10	1	0	−1
	45	5	5	1	0	86	9	1	0	0
	50	5	5	1	0	76	8	1	0	0
Projected Unit Credit, Minimum ERISA	0	—	—	4	8	0	3	12	17	0
	5	9	9	4	6	46	5	10	14	−23
	10	7	7	3	3	85	6	6	9	−40
	15	6	6	2	2	108	8	4	0	−53
	20	5	5	2	1	116	10	2	−1	−35
	25	5	5	2	1	116	11	2	0	−22

Year								
30	5	5	1	1	111	11	2	1	−13
35	5	5	1	0	104	10	2	1	−7
40	5	5	1	0	94	10	1	1	−4
45	5	5	1	0	83	9	1	1	−2
50	5	5	1	0	73	8	1	1	−2

				Beginning of Year			Application of SFAS 87 Standards	
Funding Method	Year	Expected Trend	Actual Trend	Normal cost	Fund	Benefit Payments	End-of-Year Contribution	Expense	Prepaid/(accrued) expense[a]
Aggregate	0	—	—	$20	$ 0	$ 3	$22	$17	$ 0
	5	9%	9%	11	84	5	12	12	16
	10	7	7	2	132	6	2	6	8
	15	6	6	−1	150	8	0	−2	−12
	20	5	5	−4	157	10	0	−3	6
	25	5	5	−4	161	11	0	−3	21
	30	5	5	−6	162	11	0	−3	36
	35	5	5	−8	164	10	0	−4	52
	40	5	5	−10	171	10	0	−5	72
	45	5	5	−14	186	9	0	−7	99
	50	5	5	−20	212	8	0	−9	136

(continued)

TABLE B.7 (continued)

Funding Method	Year	Expected Trend	Actual Trend	Normal cost	Beginning of Year Amortization payment	Fund	Benefit Payments	End-of-Year Contribution
Unprojected Unit Credit, Maximum Deductible	0	—	—	$1	$4	$0	$3	$5
	5	0%	9%	1	7	13	5	8
	10	0	7	1	6	40	6	7
	15	0	6	1	6	57	8	8
	20	0	5	1	6	70	10	7
	25	0	5	1	6	79	11	7
	30	0	5	1	5	85	11	7
	35	0	5	1	5	94	10	6
	40	0	5	1	5	105	10	5
	45	0	5	0	4	124	9	5
	50	0	5	0	4	152	8	4
Unprojected Unit Credit, Minimum ERISA	0	—	—	1	2	0	3	3
	5	0	9	1	5	0	5	6
	10	0	7	1	7	5	6	8
	15	0	6	1	9	19	8	11
	20	0	5	1	9	37	10	11
	25	0	5	1	9	54	11	11
	30	0	5	1	6	72	11	8
	35	0	5	1	6	81	10	7
	40	0	5	1	6	93	10	7
	45	0	5	0	5	113	9	6
	50	0	5	0	4	142	8	5

[a] Prepaid/(accrued) expense is the cumulative excess/(deficiency) of cash contributions over annual SFAS 87 expense amounts.

TABLE B.8
Funding Scenarios: Illustrative Annual Values
Group F—7% Rate of Decline: Medium Trend Scenario
(millions of dollars)

Funding Method	Year	Expected Trend	Actual Trend	Normal cost	Beginning of Year Amortization payment	Fund	Benefit Payments	End-of-Year Contribution	Application of SFAS 87 Standards Expense	Prepaid/ (accrued) expense[a]
Entry Age Normal, Maximum Deductible	0	—	—	$3	$17	$0	$3	$21	$17	$0
	5	10%	10%	4	17	97	5	22	14	26
	10	9	9	3	6	174	7	10	10	34
	15	8	8	3	0	211	10	0	0	10
	20	7	7	2	0	233	12	0	-3	22
	25	6	6	2	0	250	14	0	-6	48
	30	5	5	1	0	267	14	0	-9	87
	35	5	5	1	0	292	14	0	-11	135
	40	5	5	1	0	331	13	0	-14	194
	45	5	5	1	0	392	11	0	-19	274
	50	5	5	1	0	486	10	0	-27	383
Projected Unit Credit, Maximum Deductible	0	—	—	4	14	0	3	19	17	0
	5	10	10	5	14	86	5	20	15	14
	10	9	9	4	5	157	7	11	11	15
	15	8	8	4	0	187	10	0	2	-15
	20	7	7	3	0	199	12	0	0	-12
	25	6	6	2	0	202	14	0	-2	-1

(continued)

TABLE B.8 (continued)

					Beginning of Year				Application of SFAS 87 Standards	
Funding Method	Year	Expected Trend	Actual Trend	Normal cost	Amortization payment	Fund	Benefit Payments	End-of-Year Contribution	Expense	Prepaid/ (accrued) expense[a]
Projected Unit Credit, Maximum Deductible (continued)	30	5%	5%	$2	$0	$199	$14	$0	$ −4	$ 19
	35	5	5	2	0	195	14	0	−4	39
	40	5	5	1	0	195	13	0	−5	59
	45	5	5	1	0	202	11	0	−6	84
	50	5	5	1	0	219	10	0	−8	117
Entry Age Normal, Minimum ERISA	0	—	—	3	9	0	3	13	17	0
	5	10	10	4	9	53	5	14	18	−20
	10	9	9	3	7	105	7	11	14	−36
	15	8	8	3	4	150	10	8	4	−51
	20	7	7	2	2	177	12	5	1	−32
	25	6	6	2	0	180	14	2	−1	−21
	30	5	5	1	0	171	14	0	−2	−8
	35	5	5	1	0	157	14	0	−1	1
	40	5	5	1	0	142	13	0	−1	6
	45	5	5	1	0	127	11	0	−1	9
	50	5	5	1	0	114	10	0	0	12
Projected Unit Credit, Minimum ERISA	0	—	—	4	8	0	3	12	17	0
	5	10	10	5	8	49	5	13	18	−25
	10	9	9	4	6	99	7	11	15	−44
	15	8	8	4	4	141	10	8	5	−60
	20	7	7	3	2	168	12	5	2	−41
	25	6	6	2	0	173	14	3	0	−27

Year	Expected Trend	Actual Trend	Normal cost	Fund	Benefit Payments	End-of-Year Contribution	Expense	Prepaid/(accrued) expense
30	5	5	2	0	162	14	0	-1	-16
35	5	5	2	0	144	14	0	0	-12
40	5	5	1	0	125	13	1	0	-11
45	5	5	1	0	110	11	1	1	-7
50	5	5	1	0	97	10	1	1	-4

Funding Method

Aggregate

			Beginning of Year				Application of SFAS 87 Standards	
Year	Expected Trend	Actual Trend	Normal cost	Fund	Benefit Payments	End-of-Year Contribution	Expense	Prepaid/(accrued) expense[a]
0	—	—	$20	$ 0	$ 3	$22	$17	$ 0
5	10%	10%	15	88	5	16	15	17
10	9	9	8	153	7	8	11	12
15	8	8	3	193	10	3	1	-9
20	7	7	-1	211	12	0	-1	1
25	6	6	-4	220	14	0	-3	17
30	5	5	-9	224	14	0	-6	44
35	5	5	-12	231	14	0	-6	74
40	5	5	-17	246	13	0	-8	110
45	5	5	-23	274	11	0	-11	155
50	5	5	-32	319	10	0	-15	217

(continued)

TABLE B.8 (continued)

Funding Method	Year	Expected Trend	Actual Trend	Normal cost	Beginning of Year Amortization payment	Fund	Benefit Payments	End-of-Year Contribution
Unprojected Unit Credit, Maximum Deductible	0	—	—	$1	$4	$0	$3	$5
	5	0%	10%	1	7	13	5	8
	10	0	9	1	6	41	7	8
	15	0	8	1	8	60	10	10
	20	0	7	1	9	79	12	11
	25	0	6	1	9	96	14	11
	30	0	5	1	8	109	14	9
	35	0	5	1	7	121	14	8
	40	0	5	1	6	136	13	7
	45	0	5	1	5	159	11	6
	50	0	5	1	5	194	10	6
Unprojected Unit Credit, Minimum ERISA	0	—	—	1	2	0	3	3
	5	0	10	1	5	0	5	6
	10	0	9	1	7	5	7	9
	15	0	8	1	11	20	10	13
	20	0	7	1	12	41	12	14
	25	0	6	1	13	64	14	15
	30	0	5	1	10	88	14	11
	35	0	5	1	9	103	14	10
	40	0	5	1	7	120	13	9
	45	0	5	1	7	145	11	8
	50	0	5	1	6	181	10	7

Unit Credit with No Trend or Discount Rate, Maximum Deductible	0	—	—	2	9	0	3	12
	5	0	10	2	10	47	5	14
	10	0	9	3	7	108	7	11
	15	0	8	3	2	155	10	6
	20	0	7	3	0	185	12	2
	25	0	6	3	0	191	14	1
	30	0	5	2	0	185	14	0
	35	0	5	2	0	176	14	0
	40	0	5	2	0	168	13	0
	45	0	5	2	0	164	11	0
	50	0	5	2	0	166	10	0
Projected Unit Credit with 5% Cap on Trend, Maximum Deductible	0	—	—	1	7	0	3	9
	5	5	10	2	9	32	5	11
	10	5	9	2	8	76	7	10
	15	5	8	2	5	113	10	8
	20	5	7	2	4	137	12	7
	25	5	6	2	3	150	14	5
	30	5	5	2	0	152	14	1
	35	5	5	2	0	139	14	2
	40	5	5	1	0	125	13	1
	45	5	5	1	0	110	11	1
	50	5	5	1	0	97	10	1

(continued)

TABLE B.8 (continued)

Funding Method	Year	Expected Trend	Actual Trend	Normal cost	Beginning of Year Amortization payment	Fund	Benefit Payments	End-of-Year Contribution
Unit Credit with No Trend or Discount Rate, Minimum ERISA	0	—	—	$2	$5	$0	$3	$7
	5	0%	10%	2	6	22	5	9
	10	0	9	3	7	54	7	11
	15	0	8	3	8	93	10	12
	20	0	7	3	8	136	12	12
	25	0	6	3	4	172	14	7
	30	0	5	2	0	181	14	0
	35	0	5	2	0	171	14	0
	40	0	5	2	0	161	13	0
	45	0	5	2	0	154	11	0
	50	0	5	2	0	151	10	0
Projected Unit Credit with 5% Cap on Trend, Minimum ERISA	0	—	—	1	4	0	3	6
	5	5	10	2	5	12	5	8
	10	5	9	2	7	32	7	10
	15	5	8	2	9	59	10	12
	20	5	7	2	10	91	12	13
	25	5	6	2	9	124	14	12
	30	5	5	2	−2	154	14	0
	35	5	5	2	0	139	14	2
	40	5	5	1	0	125	13	1
	45	5	5	1	0	110	11	1
	50	5	5	1	0	97	10	1

[a]Prepaid/(accrued) expense is the cumulative excess/(deficiency) of cash contributions over annual SFAS 87 expense amounts.

TABLE B.9
Funding Scenarios: Illustrative Annual Values
Group F—7% Rate of Decline: High Trend Scenario
(millions of dollars)

					Beginning of Year				Application of SFAS 87 Standards	
Funding Method	Year	Expected Trend	Actual Trend	Normal cost	Amortization payment	Fund	Benefit Payments	End-of-Year Contribution	Expense	Prepaid/ (accrued) expense[a]
Entry Age Normal, Maximum Deductible	0	—	—	$3	$17	$0	$3	$21	$17	$0
	5	10%	10%	4	17	97	5	22	14	26
	10	9	9	3	0	188	7	3	9	40
	15	8	8	3	−4	237	10	0	−2	11
	20	8	8	3	0	264	14	0	0	18
	25	7	7	2	0	284	16	0	−4	30
	30	6	6	2	0	296	18	0	−7	51
	35	6	6	2	0	309	18	0	−7	87
	40	5	5	1	0	329	17	0	−12	138
	45	5	5	1	0	367	15	0	−15	204
	50	5	5	1	0	430	13	0	−21	290
Projected Unit Credit, Maximum Deductible	0	—	—	4	14	0	3	19	17	0
	5	10	10	5	14	86	5	20	15	14
	10	9	9	5	0	168	7	5	10	19
	15	8	8	4	−3	218	10	0	−1	−8
	20	8	8	4	0	238	14	0	2	−9
	25	7	7	3	0	246	16	0	−1	−7

(continued)

TABLE B.9 (continued)

				Beginning of Year						Application of SFAS 87 Standards	
Funding Method	Year	Expected Trend	Actual Trend	Normal cost	Amortization payment	Fund	Benefit Payments	End-of-Year Contribution		Expense	Prepaid/ (accrued) expense[a]
Projected Unit Credit, Maximum Deductible (continued)	30	6%	6%	$3	$0	$243	$18	$0		$ −3	$ −2
	35	6	6	2	0	234	18	0		−2	12
	40	5	5	2	0	224	17	0		−5	33
	45	5	5	2	0	219	15	0		−5	56
	50	5	5	1	0	222	13	0		−6	82
Entry Age Normal, Minimum ERISA	0	—	—	3	9	0	3	13		17	0
	5	10	10	4	9	53	5	14		18	−20
	10	9	9	3	7	113	7	11		14	−37
	15	8	8	3	3	172	10	7		2	−53
	20	8	8	3	3	212	14	7		3	−33
	25	7	7	2	0	232	16	3		0	−19
	30	6	6	2	0	236	18	0		−3	−7
	35	6	6	2	0	225	18	0		−1	4
	40	5	5	1	0	211	17	0		−4	20
	45	5	5	1	0	201	15	0		−4	38
	50	5	5	1	0	197	13	0		−4	58
Projected Unit Credit, Minimum ERISA	0	—	—	4	8	0	3	12		17	0
	5	10	10	5	8	49	5	13		18	−25
	10	9	9	5	5	105	7	11		14	−45
	15	8	8	4	3	162	10	7		3	−63
	20	8	8	4	3	200	14	7		4	−45
	25	7	7	3	0	221	16	4		1	−29

30	6	6	3		226	18	0	-2	-17
35	6	6	2		209	18	0	0	-11
40	5	5	2		189	17	0	-2	-1
45	5	5	2		170	15	0	-1	-8
50	5	5	1		154	13	0	-1	15

Funding Method: Aggregate

Year	Expected Trend	Actual Trend	Normal cost	Beginning of Year Fund	Benefit Payments	End-of-Year Contribution	Expense	Prepaid/ (accrued) expense[a]
0	—	—	$ 20	$ 0	$ 3	$ 22	$ 17	$ 0
5	10%	10%	15	88	5	16	15	17
10	9	9	7	162	7	8	11	13
15	8	8	1	220	10	0	-1	-5
20	8	8	3	241	14	2	1	-5
25	7	7	-2	257	16	0	-2	4
30	6	6	-5	259	18	0	-4	14
35	6	6	-6	257	18	0	-4	35
40	5	5	-12	256	17	0	-7	65
45	5	5	-16	265	15	0	-8	101
50	5	5	-22	286	13	0	-11	146

(continued)

TABLE B.9 (continued)

Funding Method	Year	Expected Trend	Actual Trend	Normal cost	Beginning of Year Amortization payment	Fund	Benefit Payments	End-of-Year Contribution
Unprojected Unit Credit, Maximum Deductible	0	—	—	$1	$4	$0	$3	$5
	5	0%	10%	1	7	13	5	8
	10	0	9	1	7	41	7	8
	15	0	8	1	9	61	10	11
	20	0	8	1	11	83	14	13
	25	0	7	1	12	105	16	14
	30	0	6	1	12	125	18	14
	35	0	6	1	11	145	18	13
	40	0	5	1	9	167	17	10
	45	0	5	1	7	195	15	8
	50	0	5	1	6	235	13	7
Unprojected Unit Credit, Minimum ERISA	0	—	—	1	2	0	3	3
	5	0	10	1	5	0	5	6
	10	0	9	1	8	6	7	9
	15	0	8	1	11	21	10	13
	20	0	8	1	14	43	14	16
	25	0	7	1	15	68	16	18
	30	0	6	1	13	97	18	16
	35	0	6	1	13	117	18	15
	40	0	5	1	11	142	17	13
	45	0	5	1	9	174	15	11
	50	0	5	1	8	218	13	9

[a] Prepaid/(accrued) expense is the cumulative excess/(deficiency) of cash contributions over annual SFAS 87 expense amounts.

TABLE B.10
Funding Scenarios: Illustrative Annual Values
Group H: Low Trend Scenario
(millions of dollars)

				Beginning of Year					Application of SFAS 87 Standards	
Funding Method	Year	Expected Trend	Actual Trend	Normal cost	Amortization payment	Fund	Benefit Payments	End-of-Year Contribution	Expense	Prepaid/ (accrued) expense[a]
Entry Age Normal, Maximum Deductible	0	—	—	$11	$8	$ 0	$ 0	$20	$14	$ 0
	5	9%	9%	13	1	116	1	15	12	32
	10	7	7	12	−5	196	2	0	7	7
	15	6	6	13	0	251	5	0	9	−33
	20	5	5	15	0	306	9	7	9	−69
	25	5	5	21	1	444	16	23	17	−46
	30	5	5	29	1	650	25	32	26	−14
	35	5	5	41	2	933	39	46	39	19
	40	5	5	58	3	1,319	58	65	56	59
	45	5	5	82	3	1,864	80	92	80	108
	50	5	5	116	4	2,633	114	128	114	169
Projected Unit Credit, Maximum Deductible	0	—	—	10	5	0	0	16	14	0
	5	9	9	12	1	97	1	14	14	9
	10	7	7	11	−5	177	2	0	8	−18
	15	6	6	13	0	230	5	0	10	−63
	20	5	5	14	0	287	9	14	9	−101
	25	5	5	20	0	434	16	21	16	−75

(continued)

TABLE B.10 (continued)

Funding Method	Year	Expected Trend	Actual Trend	Normal cost	Amortization payment	Fund	Benefit Payments	End-of-Year Contribution	Expense	Prepaid/(accrued) expense[a]
Projected Unit Credit, Maximum Deductible (continued)	30	5%	5%	$ 28	$ 0	$ 639	$ 25	$ 29	$ 26	$ −53
	35	5	5	40	0	918	39	41	38	−35
	40	5	5	56	0	1,298	58	59	56	−18
	45	5	5	80	0	1,827	80	83	80	−5
	50	5	5	113	−1	2,576	114	116	113	10
Entry Age Normal, Minimum ERISA	0	—	—	11	4	0	0	17	14	0
	5	9	9	13	2	100	1	16	13	16
	10	7	7	12	−3	196	2	0	7	8
	15	6	6	13	0	251	5	0	9	−32
	20	5	5	15	0	306	9	7	9	−68
	25	5	5	21	1	444	16	23	17	−46
	30	5	5	29	1	648	25	32	26	−16
	35	5	5	41	2	930	39	46	39	15
	40	5	5	58	3	1,313	58	65	57	53
	45	5	5	82	3	1,857	80	92	81	100
	50	5	5	116	4	2,624	114	128	114	160
Projected Unit Credit, Minimum ERISA	0	—	—	10	3	0	0	13	14	0
	5	9	9	12	1	87	1	14	14	−2
	10	7	7	11	−3	177	2	0	8	−18
	15	6	6	13	0	230	5	0	10	−63
	20	5	5	14	0	287	9	14	9	−101
	25	5	5	20	0	434	16	21	16	−74

30	5	5	28	0	639	25	29	26	−53
35	5	5	40	0	918	39	41	38	−35
40	5	5	56	0	1,298	58	59	56	−18
45	5	5	80	0	1,827	80	83	80	−4
50	5	5	113	0	2,577	114	116	113	11

				Beginning of Year				Application of SFAS 87 Standards	
Funding Method	Year	Expected Trend	Actual Trend	Normal cost	Fund	Benefit Payments	End-of-Year Contribution	Expense	Prepaid/ (accrued) expense[a]
Aggregate	0	—	—	$15	$ 0	$ 0	$16	$14	$ 0
	5	9%	9%	14	97	1	15	14	12
	10	7	7	8	195	2	0	7	7
	15	6	6	10	249	5	0	9	−34
	20	5	5	12	304	9	9	9	−70
	25	5	5	19	433	16	20	18	−57
	30	5	5	28	619	25	30	28	−46
	35	5	5	40	875	39	43	43	−40
	40	5	5	57	1,222	58	61	63	−40
	45	5	5	82	1,709	80	87	91	−50
	50	5	5	116	2,399	114	124	130	−68

(continued)

TABLE B.10 (continued)

Funding Method	Year	Expected Trend	Actual Trend	Normal cost	Beginning of Year Amortization payment	Fund	Benefit Payments	End-of-Year Contribution
Unprojected Unit Credit, Maximum Deductible	0	—	—	$1	$1	$ 0	$ 0	$ 2
	5	0%	9%	2	1	14	1	3
	10	0	7	3	2	39	2	5
	15	0	6	4	4	73	5	9
	20	0	5	6	7	126	9	13
	25	0	5	8	10	198	16	20
	30	0	5	11	16	301	25	29
	35	0	5	16	24	445	39	42
	40	0	5	22	35	640	58	61
	45	0	5	32	48	919	80	85
	50	0	5	45	67	1,318	114	119
Unprojected Unit Credit, Minimum ERISA	0	—	—	1	0	0	0	1
	5	0	9	2	1	12	1	2
	10	0	7	3	2	33	2	5
	15	0	6	4	4	65	5	9
	20	0	5	6	7	112	9	13
	25	0	5	8	11	179	16	20
	30	0	5	11	15	274	25	29
	35	0	5	16	23	404	39	42
	40	0	5	22	34	579	58	60
	45	0	5	32	48	832	80	85
	50	0	5	45	67	1,196	114	120

[a] Prepaid/(accrued) expense is the cumulative excess/(deficiency) of cash contributions over annual SFAS 87 expense amounts.

TABLE B.11
Funding Scenarios: Illustrative Annual Values
Group H: Medium Trend Scenario
(millions of dollars)

Funding Method	Year	Expected Trend	Actual Trend	Normal cost	Amortization payment	Fund	Benefit Payments	End-of-Year Contribution	Expense	Prepaid/ (accrued) expense[a]
Entry Age Normal, Maximum Deductible	0	—	—	$11	$8	$ 0	$ 0	$ 20	$ 14	$ 0
	5	10%	10%	18	7	128	1	28	19	37
	10	9	9	22	0	262	2	23	20	37
	15	8	8	26	0	385	6	28	22	−8
	20	7	7	30	0	531	12	32	22	−59
	25	6	6	34	0	694	21	37	25	−103
	30	5	5	38	0	867	33	41	27	−150
	35	5	5	54	2	1,237	51	60	46	−81
	40	5	5	77	3	1,743	77	86	71	−9
	45	5	5	109	4	2,463	106	121	104	72
	50	5	5	153	5	3,478	150	169	149	166
Projected Unit Credit, Maximum Deductible	0	—	—	10	5	0	0	16	14	0
	5	10	10	17	5	107	1	24	20	12
	10	9	9	20	0	232	2	22	21	0
	15	8	8	24	0	356	6	26	23	−47
	20	7	7	29	0	503	12	30	24	−102
	25	6	6	33	0	669	21	35	26	−152

(continued)

TABLE B.11 (continued)

				Beginning of Year					Application of SFAS 87 Standards	
Funding Method	Year	Expected Trend	Actual Trend	Normal cost	Amortization payment	Fund	Benefit Payments	End-of-Year Contribution	Expense	Prepaid/ (accrued) expense[a]
Projected Unit Credit, Maximum Deductible (continued)	30	5%	5%	$38	$0	$846	$33	$39	$27	$ −206
	35	5	5	53	0	1,216	51	55	45	−151
	40	5	5	75	0	1,718	77	78	69	−106
	45	5	5	106	−1	2,420	106	109	103	−69
	50	5	5	150	−1	3,412	150	154	148	−35
Entry Age Normal, Minimum ERISA	0	—	—	11	4	0	0	17	14	0
	5	10	10	18	4	108	1	24	20	17
	10	9	9	22	0	259	2	24	20	34
	15	8	8	26	0	385	6	28	22	−7
	20	7	7	30	0	531	12	32	22	−58
	25	6	6	34	0	694	21	37	25	−103
	30	5	5	38	0	867	33	41	27	−150
	35	5	5	54	1	1,236	51	59	46	−82
	40	5	5	77	3	1,738	77	86	71	−14
	45	5	5	109	4	2,454	106	121	104	63
	50	5	5	153	5	3,466	150	170	150	153
Projected Unit Credit, Minimum ERISA	0	—	—	10	3	0	0	13	14	0
	5	10	10	17	3	93	1	21	22	−3
	10	9	9	20	0	231	2	22	22	−1
	15	8	8	24	0	356	6	26	23	−46
	20	7	7	29	0	503	12	30	24	−101
	25	6	6	33	0	669	21	35	26	−152

30	5	5	38	0	846	33	39	27	−206
35	5	5	53	0	1,216	51	55	45	−151
40	5	5	75	0	1,718	77	78	69	−105
45	5	5	106	0	2,420	106	109	103	−69
50	5	5	150	−1	3,412	150	154	148	−35

Application of SFAS 87 Standards

Funding Method	Year	Expected Trend	Actual Trend	Normal cost	Beginning of Year Fund	Benefit Payments	End-of-Year Contribution	Expense	Prepaid/ (accrued) expense[a]
Aggregate	0	—	—	$15	$ 0	$ 0	$16	$14	$ 0
	5	10%	10%	22	104	1	24	21	13
	10	9	9	22	252	2	24	20	27
	15	8	8	25	384	6	26	22	−8
	20	7	7	28	531	12	30	23	−58
	25	6	6	31	694	21	33	25	−103
	30	5	5	33	867	33	35	28	−150
	35	5	5	50	1,204	51	53	49	−115
	40	5	5	73	1,660	77	78	77	−95
	45	5	5	105	2,303	106	112	115	−91
	50	5	5	150	3,215	150	161	168	−104

(continued)

TABLE B.11 (continued)

Funding Method	Year	Expected Trend	Actual Trend	Normal cost	Beginning of Year Amortization payment	Fund	Benefit Payments	End-of-Year Contribution
Unprojected Unit Credit, Maximum Deductible	0	—	—	$1	$1	$0	$0	$2
	5	0%	10%	2	1	14	1	3
	10	0	9	3	2	40	2	6
	15	0	8	5	6	79	6	11
	20	0	7	7	11	146	12	19
	25	0	6	11	17	250	21	29
	30	0	5	15	23	396	33	40
	35	0	5	21	31	592	51	56
	40	0	5	29	46	852	77	80
	45	0	5	42	64	1,223	106	113
	50	0	5	59	89	1,754	150	158
Unprojected Unit Credit, Minimum ERISA	0	—	—	1	0	0	0	1
	5	0	10	2	1	12	1	3
	10	0	9	3	2	34	2	5
	15	0	8	5	5	70	6	11
	20	0	7	7	10	128	12	18
	25	0	6	11	16	220	21	29
	30	0	5	15	23	354	33	40
	35	0	5	21	32	534	51	57
	40	0	5	29	45	771	77	80
	45	0	5	42	64	1,108	106	113
	50	0	5	59	89	1,592	150	159

Unit Credit with No Trend or Discount Rate, Maximum Deductible	0	—	—	4	2	0	0	7
	5	0	10	7	3	49	1	11
	10	0	9	12	3	139	2	16
	15	0	8	19	3	282	6	23
	20	0	7	29	0	502	12	31
	25	0	6	42	−1	794	21	36
	30	0	5	59	−3	1,165	33	39
	35	0	5	83	−4	1,664	51	55
	40	0	5	118	−6	2,347	77	78
	45	0	5	168	−8	3,307	106	111
	50	0	5	236	−12	4,666	150	156
Projected Unit Credit with 5% Cap on Trend, Maximum Deductible	0	—	—	2	1	0	0	4
	5	5	10	5	2	32	1	7
	10	5	9	8	3	90	2	11
	15	5	8	12	4	184	6	18
	20	5	7	18	6	331	12	26
	25	5	6	27	6	548	21	35
	30	5	5	38	1	843	33	41
	35	5	5	53	0	1,216	51	55
	40	5	5	75	0	1,718	77	78
	45	5	5	106	−1	2,420	106	109
	50	5	5	150	−1	3,412	150	154

(continued)

TABLE B.11 (continued)

					Beginning of Year			
Funding Method	Year	Expected Trend	Actual Trend	Normal cost	Amortization payment	Fund	Benefit Payments	End-of-Year Contribution
Unit Credit with No Trend or Discount Rate, Minimum ERISA	0	—	—	$ 4	$1	$ 0	$ 0	$ 6
	5	0%	10%	7	2	42	1	10
	10	0	9	12	3	124	2	16
	15	0	8	19	4	262	6	24
	20	0	7	29	4	483	12	34
	25	0	6	42	−1	794	21	36
	30	0	5	59	−2	1,165	33	39
	35	0	5	83	−3	1,665	51	55
	40	0	5	118	−5	2,348	77	78
	45	0	5	168	−7	3,309	106	111
	50	0	5	236	−9	4,668	150	156
Projected Unit Credit with 5% Cap on Trend, Minimum ERISA	0	—	—	2	1	0	0	4
	5	5	10	5	1	27	1	6
	10	5	9	8	3	80	2	11
	15	5	8	12	5	169	6	18
	20	5	7	18	7	312	12	27
	25	5	6	27	8	527	21	37
	30	5	5	38	5	827	33	45
	35	5	5	53	0	1,215	51	57
	40	5	5	75	0	1,718	77	78
	45	5	5	106	0	2,420	106	109
	50	5	5	150	−1	3,412	150	154

[a]Prepaid/(accrued) expense is the cumulative excess/(deficiency) of cash contributions over annual SFAS 87 expense amounts.

TABLE B.12
Funding Scenarios: Illustrative Annual Values
Group H: High Trend Scenario
(millions of dollars)

Funding Method	Year	Expected Trend	Actual Trend	Normal cost	Amortization payment	Fund	Benefit Payments	End-of-Year Contribution	Expense	Prepaid/ (accrued) expense[a]
Entry Age Normal, Maximum Deductible	0	—	—	$11	$8	$0	$0	$20	$14	$0
	5	10%	10%	18	7	128	1	28	19	37
	10	9	9	22	0	278	2	12	19	34
	15	8	8	27	−14	512	6	0	15	47
	20	8	8	43	0	713	13	46	34	−20
	25	7	7	52	0	1,009	25	9	38	−68
	30	6	6	61	0	1,455	42	0	33	−69
	35	6	6	91	1	1,910	68	98	74	−135
	40	5	5	102	1	2,325	102	110	78	−286
	45	5	5	145	3	3,265	140	158	126	−127
	50	5	5	203	6	4,601	199	224	189	39
Projected Unit Credit, Maximum Deductible	0	—	—	10	5	0	0	16	14	0
	5	10	10	17	5	107	1	24	20	12
	10	9	9	21	0	238	2	22	21	−13
	15	8	8	26	−12	467	6	0	18	−9
	20	8	8	41	0	669	13	44	37	−81
	25	7	7	49	0	956	25	15	40	−147

(continued)

159

TABLE B.12 (continued)

				Beginning of Year					Application of SFAS 87 Standards	
Funding Method	Year	Expected Trend	Actual Trend	Normal cost	Amortization payment	Fund	Benefit Payments	End-of-Year Contribution	Expense	Prepaid/ (accrued) expense[a]
Projected Unit Credit, Maximum Deductible (continued)	30	6%	6%	$ 59	$ 0	$1,401	$ 42	$ 0	$ 35	$ −163
	35	6	6	87	0	1,857	68	92	75	−248
	40	5	5	99	0	2,276	102	104	78	−426
	45	5	5	141	−1	3,204	140	145	125	−313
	50	5	5	198	−1	4,518	199	204	187	−218
Entry Age Normal, Minimum ERISA	0	—	—	11	4	0	0	17	14	0
	5	10	10	18	4	108	1	24	20	17
	10	9	9	22	0	265	2	24	19	22
	15	8	8	27	−8	511	6	0	15	48
	20	8	8	43	0	713	13	46	34	−19
	25	7	7	52	0	1,009	25	9	38	−68
	30	6	6	61	0	1,454	42	0	33	−69
	35	6	6	91	1	1,910	68	98	74	−135
	40	5	5	102	1	2,325	102	110	78	−286
	45	5	5	145	2	3,263	140	157	126	−129
	50	5	5	203	5	4,593	199	223	189	30
Projected Unit Credit, Minimum ERISA	0	—	—	10	3	0	0	13	14	0
	5	10	10	17	3	93	1	21	22	−3
	10	9	9	21	0	235	2	22	21	−16
	15	8	8	26	−7	465	6	0	18	−10
	20	8	8	41	0	669	13	44	37	−80
	25	7	7	49	0	956	25	15	40	−146

30	6	6	59	0	1,401	42	0	35	−163
35	6	6	87	0	1,857	68	92	75	−248
40	5	5	99	0	2,276	102	104	78	−426
45	5	5	141	−1	3,205	140	145	125	−313
50	5	5	198	−1	4,518	199	204	187	−217

				Beginning of Year				Application of SFAS 87 Standards	
Funding Method	Year	Expected Trend	Actual Trend	Normal cost	Fund	Benefit Payments	End-of-Year Contribution	Expense	Prepaid/(accrued) expense[a]
Aggregate	0	—	—	$15	$ 0	$ 0	$16	$14	$ 0
	5	10%	10%	22	104	1	24	21	13
	10	9	9	22	266	2	23	19	23
	15	8	8	18	511	6	0	15	47
	20	8	8	42	711	13	45	35	−21
	25	7	7	45	1,004	25	14	38	−73
	30	6	6	42	1,444	42	0	34	−79
	35	6	6	84	1,894	68	89	75	−151
	40	5	5	87	2,325	102	93	80	−285
	45	5	5	130	3,170	140	139	134	−225
	50	5	5	191	4,371	199	204	206	−200

(continued)

161

TABLE B.12 (continued)

Funding Method	Year	Expected Trend	Actual Trend	Normal cost	Beginning of Year Amortization payment	Fund	Benefit Payments	End-of-Year Contribution
Unprojected Unit Credit, Maximum Deductible	0	—	—	$1	$1	$0	$0	$2
	5	0%	10%	2	1	14	1	3
	10	0	9	3	2	40	2	6
	15	0	8	5	7	82	6	12
	20	0	8	8	13	156	13	22
	25	0	7	12	22	279	25	37
	30	0	6	19	34	470	42	57
	35	0	6	28	50	745	68	83
	40	0	5	39	65	1,116	102	111
	45	0	5	55	84	1,622	140	150
	50	0	5	78	118	2,326	199	209
Unprojected Unit Credit, Minimum ERISA	0	—	—	1	0	0	0	1
	5	0	10	2	1	12	1	3
	10	0	9	3	2	34	2	6
	15	0	8	5	6	72	6	11
	20	0	8	8	12	136	13	21
	25	0	7	12	21	243	25	36
	30	0	6	19	33	413	42	55
	35	0	6	28	49	658	68	82
	40	0	5	39	66	993	102	112
	45	0	5	55	88	1,459	140	153
	50	0	5	78	118	2,112	199	210

[a]Prepaid/(accrued) expense is the cumulative excess/(deficiency) of cash contributions over annual SFAS 87 expense amounts.

Appendix C
Funding Scenarios: Benefit Liabilities

The tables in appendix C summarize liability values for the model groups for selected years. These liability values correspond to the open group projections used to develop the values in appendix B.

Description

These benefit liabilities represent the present value of future benefits for retirees, vested employees, and nonvested employees, as indicated. For each of these classes, benefits for spouses are also included. Vested employees are defined as those employees eligible to retire (i.e., age 55 with 10 years of service).

Benefit liabilities for nonvested employees are shown on two bases:

(1) *Liability for accrued benefits* is the present value of the pro-rata share of benefits earned to date. Benefits are assumed to be earned ratably from date of hire to date of earliest eligibility for retirement.

(2) *Liability for total benefits* is the total present value of future benefits for nonvested employees, as produced by the valuation assumptions used.

The trends used to project medical care costs in these liability calculations are indicated in each table. For a given year, the indicated trend was assumed to apply in all future years, i.e., a level trend assumption is used to derive the present values in each year. This is consistent with the level trend assumptions made in calculating the funding costs presented in appendix B.

TABLE C.1
Funding Scenarios: Benefit Liabilities[a]
Group A: Low Trend Scenario
(millions of dollars)

Year	Expected Trend	Current Retirees	Vested Employees	Nonvested Employees Accrued benefits[b]	Total benefits
0	—	$ 30	$ 14	$ 41	$ 115
5	9%	41	20	64	159
10	7	50	28	68	149
15	6	69	45	85	172
20	5	94	66	93	183
25	5	141	99	128	252
30	5	212	139	176	351
35	5	310	192	246	495
40	5	446	265	348	700
45	5	629	373	492	989
50	5	883	527	695	1,395

TABLE C.2
Funding Scenarios: Benefit Liabilities[a]
Group A: Medium Trend Scenario
(millions of dollars)

Year	Expected Trend	Current Retirees	Vested Employees	Nonvested Employees Accrued benefits[b]	Total benefits
0	—	$ 30	$ 14	$ 41	$ 115
5	10%	46	24	86	224
10	9	65	42	123	286
15	8	94	70	160	344
20	7	139	111	188	392
25	6	201	151	213	433
30	5	280	185	233	465
35	5	411	255	326	655
40	5	591	351	460	927
45	5	833	494	652	1,310
50	5	1,170	698	921	1,847

[a] Benefit liabilities shown represent the present value of future benefits for the given class of employees, under the circumstances indicated.
[b] Accrued benefits are defined here as the pro-rata share of benefits earned to date, assuming benefits are earned ratably from date of hire to date of earliest eligibility for retirement.

TABLE C.3
Funding Scenarios: Benefit Liabilities[a]
Group A: High Trend Scenario
(millions of dollars)

Year	Expected Trend	Current Retirees	Vested Employees	Nonvested Employees Accrued benefits[b]	Nonvested Employees Total benefits
0	—	$ 30	$ 14	$ 41	$ 115
5	10%	46	24	86	224
10	9	66	42	125	291
15	8	99	74	169	364
20	8	167	143	267	575
25	7	255	205	316	664
30	6	382	268	370	762
35	6	586	388	542	1,125
40	5	782	465	610	1,228
45	5	1,104	654	863	1,734
50	5	1,549	924	1,219	2,446

TABLE C.4
Funding Scenarios: Benefit Liabilities[a]
Group F—2% Rate of Decline: Low Trend Scenario
(millions of dollars)

Year	Expected Trend	Current Retirees	Vested Employees	Nonvested Employees Accrued benefits[b]	Nonvested Employees Total benefits
0	—	$ 53	$ 28	$ 33	$ 64
5	9%	72	29	36	70
10	7	80	29	30	56
15	6	94	32	29	53
20	5	103	30	26	48
25	5	116	33	31	56
30	5	129	37	36	66
35	5	142	43	42	76
40	5	159	51	49	88
45	5	180	59	56	102
50	5	206	68	65	117

[a]Benefit liabilities shown represent the present value of future benefits for the given class of employees, under the circumstances indicated.
[b]Accrued benefits are defined here as the pro-rata share of benefits earned to date, assuming benefits are earned ratably from date of hire to date of earliest eligibility for retirement.

TABLE C.5
Funding Scenarios: Benefit Liabilities[a]
Group F—2% Rate of Decline: Medium Trend Scenario
(millions of dollars)

Year	Expected Trend	Current Retirees	Vested Employees	Nonvested Employees Accrued benefits[b]	Nonvested Employees Total benefits
0	—	$ 53	$ 28	$ 33	$ 64
5	10%	81	35	47	93
10	9	102	42	50	98
15	8	127	48	50	98
20	7	150	51	50	96
25	6	165	50	50	93
30	5	171	49	48	87
35	5	189	57	56	101
40	5	211	67	64	117
45	5	239	78	74	135
50	5	273	90	86	155

TABLE C.6
Funding Scenarios: Benefit Liabilities[a]
Group F—2% Rate of Decline: High Trend Scenario
(millions of dollars)

Year	Expected Trend	Current Retirees	Vested Employees	Nonvested Employees Accrued benefits[b]	Nonvested Employees Total benefits
0	—	$ 53	$ 28	$ 33	$ 64
5	10%	81	35	47	93
10	9	104	43	51	100
15	8	134	51	53	103
20	8	179	65	69	136
25	7	207	67	72	138
30	6	231	71	74	138
35	6	267	87	90	167
40	5	279	89	85	154
45	5	316	104	98	178
50	5	361	120	113	205

[a] Benefit liabilities shown represent the present value of future benefits for the given class of employees, under the circumstances indicated.
[b] Accrued benefits are defined here as the pro-rata share of benefits earned to date, assuming benefits are earned ratably from date of hire to date of earliest eligibility for retirement.

TABLE C.7
Funding Scenarios: Benefit Liabilities[a]
Group F—7% Rate of Decline: Low Trend Scenario
(millions of dollars)

Year	Expected Trend	Current Retirees	Vested Employees	Nonvested Employees Accrued benefits[b]	Nonvested Employees Total benefits
0	—	$ 53	$ 28	$ 33	$ 64
5	9%	72	29	34	59
10	7	80	28	23	37
15	6	91	26	17	27
20	5	94	21	12	19
25	5	96	18	10	17
30	5	94	15	9	15
35	5	86	13	8	13
40	5	78	12	8	12
45	5	69	10	7	11
50	5	60	9	6	9

TABLE C.8
Funding Scenarios: Benefit Liabilities[a]
Group F—7% Rate of Decline: Medium Trend Scenario
(millions of dollars)

Year	Expected Trend	Current Retirees	Vested Employees	Nonvested Employees Accrued benefits[b]	Nonvested Employees Total benefits
0	—	$ 53	$ 28	$ 33	$ 64
5	10%	81	35	44	79
10	9	102	41	38	65
15	8	123	40	30	50
20	7	136	35	23	37
25	6	136	27	17	27
30	5	124	20	12	20
35	5	114	18	11	18
40	5	103	16	10	16
45	5	91	14	9	14
50	5	80	12	8	13

[a]Benefit liabilities shown represent the present value of future benefits for the given class of employees, under the circumstances indicated.
[b]Accrued benefits are defined here as the pro-rata share of benefits earned to date, assuming benefits are earned ratably from date of hire to date of earliest eligibility for retirement.

TABLE C.9
Funding Scenarios: Benefit Liabilities[a]
Group F—7% Rate of Decline: High Trend Scenario
(millions of dollars)

				Nonvested Employees	
Year	Expected Trend	Current Retirees	Vested Employees	Accrued benefits[b]	Total benefits
0	—	$ 53	$ 28	$ 33	$ 64
5	10%	81	35	44	79
10	9	104	41	39	66
15	8	130	42	32	53
20	8	163	44	31	52
25	7	170	36	24	40
30	6	166	29	19	31
35	6	161	27	18	29
40	5	136	21	13	21
45	5	121	18	12	19
50	5	106	16	10	17

TABLE C.10
Funding Scenarios: Benefit Liabilities[a]
Group H: Low Trend Scenario
(millions of dollars)

				Nonvested Employees	
Year	Expected Trend	Current Retirees	Vested Employees	Accrued benefits[b]	Total benefits
0	—	$ 0	$ 1	$ 53	$ 226
5	9%	9	17	109	284
10	7	28	51	101	226
15	6	62	74	121	250
20	5	103	94	138	266
25	5	171	135	196	374
30	5	264	216	252	501
35	5	398	303	345	701
40	5	596	384	497	1,013
45	5	831	538	715	1,443
50	5	1,153	776	1,014	2,028

[a]Benefit liabilities shown represent the present value of future benefits for the given class of employees, under the circumstances indicated.
[b]Accrued benefits are defined here as the pro-rata share of benefits earned to date, assuming benefits are earned ratably from date of hire to date of earliest eligibility for retirement.

TABLE C.11
Funding Scenarios: Benefit Liabilities[a]
Group H: Medium Trend Scenario
(millions of dollars)

Year	Expected Trend	Current Retirees	Vested Employees	Nonvested Employees Accrued benefits[b]	Nonvested Employees Total benefits
0	—	$ 0	$ 1	$ 53	$ 226
5	10%	11	20	148	403
10	9	36	75	189	451
15	8	86	116	237	519
20	7	154	160	286	589
25	6	245	206	330	650
30	5	350	287	334	663
35	5	527	402	457	929
40	5	790	509	658	1,342
45	5	1,101	712	947	1,910
50	5	1,527	1,028	1,342	2,685

TABLE C.12
Funding Scenarios: Benefit Liabilities[a]
Group H: High Trend Scenario
(millions of dollars)

Year	Expected Trend	Current Retirees	Vested Employees	Nonvested Employees Accrued benefits[b]	Nonvested Employees Total benefits
0	—	$ 0	$ 1	$ 53	$ 226
5	10%	11	20	148	403
10	9	37	76	193	459
15	8	90	123	251	549
20	8	186	208	413	878
25	7	312	281	496	1,012
30	6	477	420	537	1,104
35	6	751	614	773	1,624
40	5	1,046	673	871	1,777
45	5	1,458	943	1,254	2,530
50	5	2,023	1,361	1,778	3,556

[a]Benefit liabilities shown represent the present value of future benefits for the given class of employees, under the circumstances indicated.
[b]Accrued benefits are defined here as the pro-rata share of benefits earned to date, assuming benefits are earned ratably from date of hire to date of earliest eligibility for retirement.

Appendix D
Funding Scenarios:
Illustrative Funding Ratios

Appendix D includes tables summarizing the funding ratios generated under each of the funding scenarios presented in appendix B.

Description

Following is a description of the values included in each table:

(1) *Expected trend* is the trend assumed to apply for all future years, in the given year's actuarial valuation. In other words, for the given funding method and trend scenario, the indicated trends were used in deriving funding costs each year. These trends correspond to the expected trend values shown in appendix B.

(2) *Funding ratios* represent the proportion of the present value of future benefits, for a given class of employees, that is currently funded. To determine these ratios, the current fund is allocated to classes of employees in the following order of priority:

(a) current retirees;
(b) vested employees (those currently eligible to retire); and
(c) nonvested employees.

The fund is first allocated to cover the benefit liability for the current retirees. Any remaining amounts are allocated to cover the benefit liability of vested employees first, and then the nonvested employees. The applicable benefit liabilities are presented in appendix C.

The tables are presented in the following order:
Group A
Group F—2 % Rate of Decline
Group F—7% Rate of Decline
Group H

For each group, there is a low, medium, and high trend scenario; for each trend scenario, a range of funding scenarios are presented, distinguished by different funding methods.

TABLE D.1
Funding Scenarios: Illustrative Funding Ratios[a]
Group A: Low Trend Scenario

Funding Method	Year	Expected Trend	Current Retirees	Vested Employees	Nonvested Employees Accrued benefits[b]	Nonvested Employees Total benefits
Entry Age Normal, Maximum Deductible	0	—	0%	0%	0%	0%
	5	9%	100	100	68	27
	10	7	100	100	100	69
	15	6	100	100	100	64
	20	5	100	100	100	59
	25	5	100	100	87	44
	30	5	100	100	85	43
	35	5	100	100	85	42
	40	5	100	100	86	43
	45	5	100	100	86	43
	50	5	100	100	87	43
Projected Unit Credit, Maximum Deductible	0	—	0	0	0	0
	5	9	100	100	32	13
	10	7	100	100	100	48
	15	6	100	100	83	41
	20	5	100	100	66	34
	25	5	100	100	65	33
	30	5	100	100	65	33
	35	5	100	100	65	32
	40	5	100	100	65	32
	45	5	100	100	65	33
	50	5	100	100	65	33

Entry Age Normal, Minimum
ERISA

0	0	—	0	0	0
5	5	9	100	100	21	8
10	10	7	100	100	100	54
15	15	6	100	100	100	57
20	20	5	100	100	99	50
25	25	5	100	100	86	44
30	30	5	100	100	85	42
35	35	5	100	100	85	42
40	40	5	100	100	85	42
45	45	5	100	100	86	43
50	50	5	100	100	86	43

Projected Unit Credit, Minimum
ERISA

0	0	—	0	0	0	0
5	5	9	100	89	0	0
10	10	7	100	100	75	34
15	15	6	100	100	82	40
20	20	5	100	100	66	34
25	25	5	100	100	65	33
30	30	5	100	100	65	33
35	35	5	100	100	65	32
40	40	5	100	100	65	32
45	45	5	100	100	65	33
50	50	5	100	100	65	33

(continued)

TABLE D.1 (continued)

Funding Method	Year	Expected Trend	Current Retirees	Vested Employees	Nonvested Employees Accrued benefits[b]	Total benefits
Aggregate	0	—	0%	0%	0%	0%
	5	9%	100	100	27	11
	10	7	100	100	100	54
	15	6	100	100	100	57
	20	5	100	100	97	49
	25	5	100	100	80	40
	30	5	100	100	73	36
	35	5	100	100	69	34
	40	5	100	100	67	33
	45	5	100	100	66	33
	50	5	100	100	65	32
Unprojected Unit Credit, Maximum Deductible	0	—	0	0	0	0
	5	0	19	0	0	0
	10	0	53	0	0	0
	15	0	66	0	0	0
	20	0	74	0	0	0
	25	0	73	0	0	0
	30	0	71	0	0	0
	35	0	71	0	0	0
	40	0	73	0	0	0
	45	0	76	0	0	0
	50	0	78	0	0	0

Unprojected Unit Credit, Minimum ERISA					
0	0	—	0	0	0
5	5	0	0	0	0
10	10	0	21	0	0
15	15	0	40	0	0
20	20	0	56	0	0
25	25	0	61	0	0
30	30	0	62	0	0
35	35	0	61	0	0
40	40	0	63	0	0
45	45	0	66	0	0
50	50	0	68	0	0

[a] Funding ratios shown reflect the proportion of the present value of future benefits, for the given class of employees, that is covered by the current fund.
[b] Accrued benefits are defined here as the pro-rata share of benefits earned to date, assuming benefits are earned ratably from date of hire to date of earliest eligibility for retirement.

TABLE D.2
Funding Scenarios: Illustrative Funding Ratios[a]
Group A: Medium Trend Scenario

Funding Method	Year	Expected Trend	Current Retirees	Vested Employees	Nonvested Employees Accrued benefits[b]	Nonvested Employees Total benefits
Entry Age Normal, Maximum Deductible	0	—	0%	0%	0%	0%
	5	9%	100	100	52	20
	10	7	100	100	100	45
	15	6	100	100	99	46
	20	5	100	100	94	45
	25	5	100	100	90	44
	30	5	100	100	87	44
	35	5	100	100	85	42
	40	5	100	100	85	42
	45	5	100	100	86	43
	50	5	100	100	86	43
Projected Unit Credit, Maximum Deductible	0	—	0	0	0	0
	5	9	100	100	21	8
	10	7	100	100	67	29
	15	6	100	100	69	32
	20	5	100	100	67	32
	25	5	100	100	66	32
	30	5	100	100	65	33
	35	5	100	100	65	32
	40	5	100	100	65	32
	45	5	100	100	65	33
	50	5	100	100	65	33

Entry Age Normal, Minimum

ERISA					
0	—	0	0	0	0
5	9	100	100	11	4
10	7	100	100	70	30
15	6	100	100	99	46
20	5	100	100	94	45
25	5	100	100	90	44
30	5	100	100	87	44
35	5	100	100	85	42
40	5	100	100	85	42
45	5	100	100	85	42
50	5	100	100	85	42

Projected Unit Credit, Minimum

ERISA					
0	—	0	0	0	0
5	9	100	69	0	0
10	7	100	100	39	17
15	6	100	100	69	32
20	5	100	100	67	32
25	5	100	100	66	32
30	5	100	100	65	33
35	5	100	100	65	32
40	5	100	100	65	32
45	5	100	100	65	33
50	5	100	100	65	33

(continued)

TABLE D.2 (continued)

Funding Method	Year	Expected Trend	Current Retirees	Vested Employees	Nonvested Employees Accrued benefits[b]	Nonvested Employees Total benefits
Aggregate	0	—	0%	0%	0%	0%
	5	9%	100	100	16	6
	10	7	100	100	71	31
	15	6	100	100	96	45
	20	5	100	100	94	45
	25	5	100	100	90	44
	30	5	100	100	87	43
	35	5	100	100	77	38
	40	5	100	100	72	36
	45	5	100	100	69	34
	50	5	100	100	67	33
Unprojected Unit Credit, Maximum Deductible	0	—	0	0	0	0
	5	0	17	0	0	0
	10	0	42	0	0	0
	15	0	52	0	0	0
	20	0	58	0	0	0
	25	0	64	0	0	0
	30	0	70	0	0	0
	35	0	71	0	0	0
	40	0	73	0	0	0
	45	0	76	0	0	0
	50	0	78	0	0	0

Unprojected Unit Credit, Minimum ERISA

0	0	—	0	0	0
5	5	0	4	0	0
10	10	0	17	0	0
15	15	0	32	0	0
20	20	0	44	0	0
25	25	0	52	0	0
30	30	0	59	0	0
35	35	0	61	0	0
40	40	0	63	0	0
45	45	0	66	0	0
50	50	0	68	0	0

Unit Credit with No Trend or Discount Rate, Maximum Deductible

0	0	—	0	0	0
5	5	0	94	0	0
10	10	0	100	100	9	4
15	15	0	100	100	37	17
20	20	0	100	100	67	32
25	25	0	100	100	100	52
30	30	0	100	100	100	79
35	35	0	100	100	100	79
40	40	0	100	100	100	79
45	45	0	100	100	100	79
50	50	0	100	100	100	78

Projected Unit Credit with 5% Cap on Trend, Maximum Deductible

0	0	—	0	0	0
5	5	5	62	0	0
10	10	5	100	33	0
15	15	5	100	81	0
20	20	5	100	100	3	2
25	25	5	100	100	27	13

(continued)

TABLE D.2 (continued)

Funding Method	Year	Expected Trend	Current Retirees	Vested Employees	Nonvested Employees Accrued benefits[b]	Total benefits
Projected Unit Credit with 5% Cap on Trend, Maximum Deductible (continued)	30%	5%	100%	100%	64%	32%
	35	5	100	100	65	32
	40	5	100	100	65	32
	45	5	100	100	65	33
	50	5	100	100	65	33
Unit Credit with No Trend or Discount Rate, Minimum ERISA	0	—	0	0	0	0
	5	0	0	0	0	0
	10	0	60	45	0	0
	15	0	100	100	11	5
	20	0	100	100	49	24
	25	0	100	100	100	51
	30	0	100	100	100	79
	35	0	100	100	100	79
	40	0	100	100	100	79
	45	0	100	100	100	79
	50	0	100	100	100	79
Projected Unit Credit with 5% Cap on Trend, Minimum ERISA	0	—	0	0	0	0
	5	5	36	0	0	0
	10	5	80	0	0	0
	15	5	100	33	0	0
	20	5	100	77	0	0
	25	5	100	100	15	8

180

30	5	100	100	60	30
35	5	100	100	65	32
40	5	100	100	65	32
45	5	100	100	65	33
50	5	100	100	65	33

[a] Funding ratios shown reflect the proportion of the present value of future benefits, for the given class of employees, that is covered by the current fund.
[b] Accrued benefits are defined here as the pro-rata share of benefits earned to date, assuming benefits are earned ratably from date of hire to date of earliest eligibility for retirement.

TABLE D.3
Funding Scenarios: Illustrative Funding Ratios[a]
Group A: High Trend Scenario

Funding Method	Year	Expected Trend	Current Retirees	Vested Employees	Nonvested Employees Accrued benefits[b]	Nonvested Employees Total benefits
Entry Age Normal, Maximum Deductible	0	—	0%	0%	0%	0%
	5	9%	100	100	52	20
	10	7	100	100	100	47
	15	6	100	100	100	69
	20	5	100	100	97	45
	25	5	100	100	100	49
	30	5	100	100	100	61
	35	5	100	100	89	43
	40	5	100	100	87	43
	45	5	100	100	86	43
	50	5	100	100	85	43
Projected Unit Credit, Maximum Deductible	0	—	0	0	0	0
	5	9	100	100	21	8
	10	7	100	100	70	30
	15	6	100	100	100	49
	20	5	100	100	67	31
	25	5	100	100	70	33
	30	5	100	100	94	46
	35	5	100	100	66	32
	40	5	100	100	65	32
	45	5	100	100	65	33
	50	5	100	100	65	33

Entry Age Normal, Minimum

ERISA	0	—	0	0	0	0
	5	9	100	100	11	4
	10	7	100	100	80	34
	15	6	100	100	100	61
	20	5	100	100	97	45
	25	5	100	100	100	49
	30	5	100	100	100	61
	35	5	100	100	89	43
	40	5	100	100	87	43
	45	5	100	100	86	43
	50	5	100	100	85	42

Projected Unit Credit, Minimum

ERISA	0	—	0	0	0	0
	5	9	100	69	0	0
	10	7	100	100	47	20
	15	6	100	100	89	41
	20	5	100	100	67	31
	25	5	100	100	70	33
	30	5	100	100	94	46
	35	5	100	100	66	32
	40	5	100	100	65	32
	45	5	100	100	65	33
	50	5	100	100	65	33

(continued)

TABLE D.3 (continued)

Funding Method	Year	Expected Trend	Current Retirees	Vested Employees	Nonvested Employees Accrued benefits[b]	Total benefits
Aggregate	0	—	0%	0%	0%	0%
	5	9%	100	100	16	6
	10	7	100	100	82	35
	15	6	100	100	100	60
	20	5	100	100	95	44
	25	5	100	100	100	48
	30	5	100	100	100	59
	35	5	100	100	86	42
	40	5	100	100	87	43
	45	5	100	100	78	39
	50	5	100	100	72	36
Unprojected Unit Credit, Maximum Deductible	0	—	0	0	0	0
	5	0	17	0	0	0
	10	0	42	0	0	0
	15	0	51	0	0	0
	20	0	51	0	0	0
	25	0	56	0	0	0
	30	0	61	0	0	0
	35	0	63	0	0	0
	40	0	72	0	0	0
	45	0	75	0	0	0
	50	0	78	0	0	0

Unprojected Unit Credit, Minimum ERISA			
0	—	0	0
5	0	4	0
10	0	17	0
15	0	31	0
20	0	38	0
25	0	45	0
30	0	50	0
35	0	52	0
40	0	61	0
45	0	65	0
50	0	67	0

[a] Funding ratios shown reflect the proportion of the present value of future benefits, for the given class of employees, that is covered by the current fund.
[b] Accrued benefits are defined here as the pro-rata share of benefits earned to date, assuming benefits are earned ratably from date of hire to date of earliest eligibility for retirement.

TABLE D.4
Funding Scenarios: Illustrative Funding Ratios[a]
Group F—2% Rate of Decline: Low Trend Scenario

Funding Method	Year	Expected Trend	Current Retirees	Vested Employees	Nonvested Employees Accrued benefits[b]	Nonvested Employees Total benefits
Entry Age Normal, Maximum Deductible	0	—	0%	0%	0%	0%
	5	9%	100	70	0	0
	10	7	100	100	100	84
	15	6	100	100	100	94
	20	5	100	100	100	100
	25	5	100	100	100	85
	30	5	100	100	94	52
	35	5	100	100	94	52
	40	5	100	100	95	52
	45	5	100	100	94	52
	50	5	100	100	94	52
Projected Unit Credit, Maximum Deductible	0	—	0	0	0	0
	5	9	100	32	0	0
	10	7	100	100	100	55
	15	6	100	100	99	53
	20	5	100	100	100	56
	25	5	100	100	62	34
	30	5	100	100	63	34
	35	5	100	100	63	34
	40	5	100	100	63	34
	45	5	100	100	63	34
	50	5	100	100	63	34

Entry Age Normal, Minimum
ERISA

0	—	0	0	0	0
5	9	73	0	0	0
10	7	100	77	0	0
15	6	100	100	46	25
20	5	100	100	92	50
25	5	100	100	92	50
30	5	100	100	93	51
35	5	100	100	94	52
40	5	100	100	93	51
45	5	100	100	94	52
50	5	100	100	94	52

Projected Unit Credit, Minimum
ERISA

0	—	0	0	0	0
5	9	67	0	0	0
10	7	100	48	0	0
15	6	100	100	10	5
20	5	100	100	60	32
25	5	100	100	61	33
30	5	100	100	63	34
35	5	100	100	63	34
40	5	100	100	63	34
45	5	100	100	63	34
50	5	100	100	63	34

(continued)

TABLE D.4 (continued)

Funding Method	Year	Expected Trend	Current Retirees	Vested Employees	Nonvested Employees Accrued benefits[b]	Total benefits
Aggregate	0	—	0%	0%	0%	0%
	5	9%	100	51	0	0
	10	7	100	100	100	64
	15	6	100	100	100	80
	20	5	100	100	100	95
	25	5	100	100	100	60
	30	5	100	100	90	50
	35	5	100	100	87	48
	40	5	100	100	85	47
	45	5	100	100	84	46
	50	5	100	100	84	46
Unprojected Unit Credit, Maximum Deductible	0	—	0	0	0	0
	5	0	18	0	0	0
	10	0	53	0	0	0
	15	0	66	0	0	0
	20	0	80	0	0	0
	25	0	87	0	0	0
	30	0	94	0	0	0
	35	0	100	11	0	0
	40	0	100	43	0	0
	45	0	100	77	0	0
	50	0	100	100	17	9

Unprojected Unit Credit, Minimum ERISA

0	0	0	0
5	—	0	0
10	0	0	0
15	0	9	0
20	0	26	0
25	0	48	0
30	0	64	0
35	0	81	0
40	0	90	0
45	0	100	1
50	0	100	12
	0	100	24

[a] Funding ratios shown reflect the proportion of the present value of future benefits, for the given class of employees, that is covered by the current fund.
[b] Accrued benefits are defined here as the pro-rata share of benefits earned to date, assuming benefits are earned ratably from date of hire to date of earliest eligibility for retirement.

TABLE D.5
Funding Scenarios: Illustrative Funding Ratios[a]
Group F—2% Rate of Decline: Medium Trend Scenario

Funding Method	Year	Expected Trend	Current Retirees	Vested Employees	Nonvested Employees Accrued benefits[b]	Nonvested Employees Total benefits
Entry Age Normal, Maximum Deductible	0	—	0%	0%	0%	0%
	5	9%	100	54	0	0
	10	7	100	100	88	45
	15	6	100	100	100	60
	20	5	100	100	100	63
	25	5	100	100	100	68
	30	5	100	100	100	75
	35	5	100	100	94	52
	40	5	100	100	94	52
	45	5	100	100	94	52
	50	5	100	100	94	52
Projected Unit Credit, Maximum Deductible	0	—	0	0	0	0
	5	9	100	19	0	0
	10	7	100	100	46	24
	15	6	100	100	63	32
	20	5	100	100	68	35
	25	5	100	100	68	36
	30	5	100	100	68	37
	35	5	100	100	63	34
	40	5	100	100	63	34
	45	5	100	100	63	34
	50	5	100	100	63	34

Entry Age Normal, Minimum
ERISA

0	—	0	0	0	0
5	9	69	0	0	0
10	7	100	44	0	0
15	6	100	100	21	11
20	5	100	100	86	45
25	5	100	100	100	53
30	5	100	100	100	62
35	5	100	100	93	51
40	5	100	100	93	51
45	5	100	100	94	52
50	5	100	100	94	52

Projected Unit Credit, Minimum
ERISA

0	—	0	0	0	0
5	9	63	0	0	0
10	7	100	18	0	0
15	6	100	88	0	0
20	5	100	100	43	23
25	5	100	100	62	33
30	5	100	100	67	37
35	5	100	100	63	34
40	5	100	100	63	34
45	5	100	100	63	34
50	5	100	100	63	34

(continued)

TABLE D.5 (continued)

Funding Method	Year	Expected Trend	Current Retirees	Vested Employees	Nonvested Employees Accrued benefits[b]	Nonvested Employees Total benefits
Aggregate	0	—	0%	0%	0%	0%
	5	9%	100	31	0	0
	10	7	100	100	49	25
	15	6	100	100	100	53
	20	5	100	100	100	63
	25	5	100	100	100	67
	30	5	100	100	100	74
	35	5	100	100	92	51
	40	5	100	100	88	49
	45	5	100	100	86	47
	50	5	100	100	85	47
Unprojected Unit Credit, Maximum Deductible	0	—	0	0	0	0
	5	0	16	0	0	0
	10	0	42	0	0	0
	15	0	52	0	0	0
	20	0	63	0	0	0
	25	0	75	0	0	0
	30	0	92	0	0	0
	35	0	100	7	0	0
	40	0	100	39	0	0
	45	0	100	72	0	0
	50	0	100	100	11	6

Unprojected Unit Credit, Minimum ERISA	0	—	0	0	0	0
	5	0	0	0	0	0
	10	0	7	0	0	0
	15	0	21	0	0	0
	20	0	37	0	0	0
	25	0	54	0	0	0
	30	0	77	0	0	0
	35	0	88	0	0	0
	40	0	100	0	0	0
	45	0	100	10	0	0
	50	0	100	22	0	0
Unit Credit with No Trend or Discount Rate, Maximum Deductible	0	—	0	0	0	0
	5	0	59	0	0	0
	10	0	100	31	0	0
	15	0	100	100	1	1
	20	0	100	100	63	33
	25	0	100	100	100	65
	30	0	100	100	100	100
	35	0	100	100	100	100
	40	0	100	100	100	100
	45	0	100	100	100	100
	50	0	100	100	100	100
Projected Unit Credit with 5% Cap on Trend, Maximim Deductible	0	—	0	0	0	0
	5	5	41	0	0	0
	10	5	79	0	0	0
	15	5	100	1	0	0
	20	5	100	39	0	0
	25	5	100	92	0	0

TABLE D.5 (continued)

Funding Method	Year	Expected Trend	Current Retirees	Vested Employees	Nonvested Employees Accrued benefits[b]	Nonvested Employees Total benefits
Projected Unit Credit with 5% Cap on Trend, Maximum Deductible (continued)	30	5%	100%	100%	66%	36%
	35	5	100	100	59	33
	40	5	100	100	59	33
	45	5	100	100	58	32
	50	5	100	100	57	31
Unit Credit with No Trend or Discount Rate, Minimum ERISA	0	—	0	0	0	0
	5	0	29	0	0	0
	10	0	59	0	0	0
	15	0	90	0	0	0
	20	0	100	65	0	0
	25	0	100	100	86	46
	30	0	100	100	100	100
	35	0	100	100	100	100
	40	0	100	100	100	100
	45	0	100	100	100	100
	50	0	100	100	100	100
Projected Unit Credit with 5% Cap on Trend, Minimum ERISA	0	—	0	0	0	0
	5	5	16	0	0	0
	10	5	35	0	0	0
	15	5	58	0	0	0
	20	5	82	0	0	0
	25	5	100	35	0	0

30	5	100	100	62	34
35	5	100	100	58	32
40	5	100	100	58	32
45	5	100	100	57	32
50	5	100	100	56	31

[a] Funding ratios shown reflect the proportion of the present value of future benefits, for the given class of employees, that is covered by the current fund.

[b] Accrued benefits are defined here as the pro-rata share of benefits earned to date, assuming benefits are earned ratably from date of hire to date of earliest eligibility for retirement.

TABLE D.6
Funding Scenarios: Illustrative Funding Ratios[a]
Group F—2% Rate of Decline: High Trend Scenario

Funding Method	Year	Expected Trend	Current Retirees	Vested Employees	Nonvested Employees Accrued benefits[b]	Nonvested Employees Total benefits
Entry Age Normal, Maximum Deductible	0	—	0%	0%	0%	0%
	5	9%	100	54	0	0
	10	7	100	100	100	56
	15	6	100	100	100	91
	20	5	100	100	100	56
	25	5	100	100	100	68
	30	5	100	100	100	82
	35	5	100	100	97	52
	40	5	100	100	100	61
	45	5	100	100	94	52
	50	5	100	100	93	51
Projected Unit Credit, Maximum Deductible	0	—	0	0	0	0
	5	9	100	19	0	0
	10	7	100	100	65	33
	15	6	100	100	100	64
	20	5	100	100	63	32
	25	5	100	100	81	42
	30	5	100	100	100	58
	35	5	100	100	63	34
	40	5	100	100	65	36
	45	5	100	100	63	34
	50	5	100	100	63	34

Entry Age Normal, Minimum

0	—	0	0	0	0
5	9	69	0	0	0
10	7	100	59	0	0
15	6	100	100	58	30
20	5	100	100	74	38
25	5	100	100	100	53

ERISA

30	5	100	100	100	82
35	5	100	100	97	52
40	5	100	100	100	61
45	5	100	100	93	52
50	5	100	100	93	51

Projected Unit Credit, Minimum

0	—	0	0	0	0
5	9	63	0	0	0
10	7	100	30	0	0
15	6	100	100	19	10
20	5	100	100	33	17
25	5	100	100	63	33

ERISA

30	5	100	100	100	58
35	5	100	100	63	34
40	5	100	100	65	36
45	5	100	100	63	34
50	5	100	100	63	34

(continued)

TABLE D.6 (continued)

Funding Method	Year	Expected Trend	Current Retirees	Vested Employees	Nonvested Employees Accrued benefits[b]	Nonvested Employees Total benefits
Aggregate	0	—	0%	0%	0%	0%
	5	9%	100	31	0	0
	10	7	100	100	65	33
	15	6	100	100	100	78
	20	5	100	100	100	52
	25	5	100	100	100	68
	30	5	100	100	100	81
	35	5	100	100	97	52
	40	5	100	100	100	60
	45	5	100	100	91	50
	50	5	100	100	87	48
Unprojected Unit Credit, Maximum Deductible	0	—	0	0	0	0
	5	0	16	0	0	0
	10	0	41	0	0	0
	15	0	51	0	0	0
	20	0	55	0	0	0
	25	0	66	0	0	0
	30	0	79	0	0	0
	35	0	88	0	0	0
	40	0	100	23	0	0
	45	0	100	59	0	0
	50	0	100	94	0	0

Unprojected Unit Credit, Minimum ERISA				
0	—	0	0	0
5	0	0	0	0
10	0	7	0	0
15	0	21	0	0
20	0	33	0	0
25	0	47	0	0
30	0	64	0	0
35	0	74	0	0
40	0	93	0	0
45	0	100	5	0
50	0	100	17	0

[a] Funding ratios shown reflect the proportion of the present value of future benefits, for the given class of employees, that is covered by the current fund.
[b] Accrued benefits are defined here as the pro-rata share of benefits earned to date, assuming benefits are earned ratably from date of hire to date of earliest eligibility for retirement.

TABLE D.7
Funding Scenarios: Illustrative Funding Ratios[a]
Group F—7% Rate of Decline: Low Trend Scenario

					Nonvested Employees	
Funding Method	Year	Expected Trend	Current Retirees	Vested Employees	Accrued benefits[b]	Total benefits
Entry Age Normal, Maximum Deductible	0	—	0%	0%	0%	0%
	5	9%	100	61	0	0
	10	7	100	100	100	100
	15	6	100	100	100	100
	20	5	100	100	100	100
	25	5	100	100	100	100
	30	5	100	100	100	100
	35	5	100	100	100	100
	40	5	100	100	100	100
	45	5	100	100	100	100
	50	5	100	100	100	100
Projected Unit Credit, Maximum Deductible	0	—	0	0	0	0
	5	9	100	26	0	0
	10	7	100	100	100	64
	15	6	100	100	100	89
	20	5	100	100	100	100
	25	5	100	100	100	100
	30	5	100	100	100	100
	35	5	100	100	100	100
	40	5	100	100	100	100
	45	5	100	100	100	100
	50	5	100	100	100	100

Entry Age Normal, Minimum ERISA

0	—	0	0	0	0
5	9	69	0	0	0
10	7	100	38	0	0
15	6	100	86	0	0
20	5	100	100	59	38
25	5	100	100	83	52
30	5	100	100	98	61
35	5	100	100	98	61
40	5	100	100	98	62
45	5	100	100	98	62
50	5	100	100	98	62

Projected Unit Credit, Minimum ERISA

0	—	0	0	0	0
5	9	64	0	0	0
10	7	100	19	0	0
15	6	100	65	0	0
20	5	100	100	9	6
25	5	100	100	13	8
30	5	100	100	26	16
35	5	100	100	51	32
40	5	100	100	60	38
45	5	100	100	60	38
50	5	100	100	60	38

(continued)

TABLE D.7 (continued)

Funding Method	Year	Expected Trend	Current Retirees	Vested Employees	Nonvested Employees Accrued benefits[b]	Nonvested Employees Total benefits
Aggregate	0	—	0%	0%	0%	0%
	5	9%	100	40	0	0
	10	7	100	100	100	66
	15	6	100	100	100	100
	20	5	100	100	100	100
	25	5	100	100	100	100
	30	5	100	100	100	100
	35	5	100	100	100	100
	40	5	100	100	100	100
	45	5	100	100	100	100
	50	5	100	100	100	100
Unprojected Unit Credit, Maximum Deductible	0	—	0	0	0	0
	5	0	18	0	0	0
	10	0	50	0	0	0
	15	0	62	0	0	0
	20	0	75	0	0	0
	25	0	82	0	0	0
	30	0	91	0	0	0
	35	0	100	54	0	0
	40	0	100	100	100	100
	45	0	100	100	100	100
	50	0	100	100	100	100

	Unprojected Unit Credit, Minimum ERISA					
0	0	—	0	0	0	0
5	5	0	0	0	0	0
10	10	0	6	0	0	0
15	15	0	20	0	0	0
20	20	0	39	0	0	0
25	25	0	56	0	0	0
30	30	0	77	0	0	0
35	35	0	93	0	0	0
40	40	0	100	45	0	0
45	45	0	100	100	100	33
50	50	0	100	100	100	100

[a] Funding ratios shown reflect the proportion of the present value of future benefits, for the given class of employees, that is covered by the current fund.
[b] Accrued benefits are defined here as the pro-rata share of benefits earned to date, assuming benefits are earned ratably from date of hire to date of earliest eligibility for retirement.

TABLE D.8
Funding Scenarios: Illustrative Funding Ratios[a]
Group F—7% Rate of Decline: Medium Trend Scenario

Funding Method	Year	Expected Trend	Current Retirees	Vested Employees	Nonvested Employees Accrued benefits[b]	Nonvested Employees Total benefits
Entry Age Normal, Maximum Deductible	0	—	0%	0%	0%	0%
	5	9%	100	45	0	0
	10	7	100	100	83	49
	15	6	100	100	100	97
	20	5	100	100	100	100
	25	5	100	100	100	100
	30	5	100	100	100	100
	35	5	100	100	100	100
	40	5	100	100	100	100
	45	5	100	100	100	100
	50	5	100	100	100	100
Projected Unit Credit, Maximum Deductible	0	—	0	0	0	0
	5	9	100	12	0	0
	10	7	100	100	37	22
	15	6	100	100	78	47
	20	5	100	100	100	76
	25	5	100	100	100	100
	30	5	100	100	100	100
	35	5	100	100	100	100
	40	5	100	100	100	100
	45	5	100	100	100	100
	50	5	100	100	100	100

Entry Age Normal, Minimum

ERISA	0	—	0	0	0	0
	5	9	65	0	0	0
	10	7	100	9	0	0
	15	6	100	66	0	0
	20	5	100	100	28	17
	25	5	100	100	100	62
	30	5	100	100	100	100
	35	5	100	100	100	100
	40	5	100	100	100	100
	45	5	100	100	100	100
	50	5	100	100	100	100

Projected Unit Credit, Minimum

ERISA	0	—	0	0	0	0
	5	9	60	0	0	0
	10	7	97	0	0	0
	15	6	100	46	0	0
	20	5	100	92	0	0
	25	5	100	100	59	36
	30	5	100	100	100	92
	35	5	100	100	100	68
	40	5	100	100	60	38
	45	5	100	100	60	38
	50	5	100	100	60	38

(continued)

TABLE D.8 (continued)

Funding Method	Year	Expected Trend	Current Retirees	Vested Employees	Nonvested Employees Accrued benefits[b]	Nonvested Employees Total benefits
Aggregate	0	—	0%	0%	0%	0%
	5	9%	100	20	0	0
	10	7	100	100	26	16
	15	6	100	100	98	59
	20	5	100	100	100	100
	25	5	100	100	100	100
	30	5	100	100	100	100
	35	5	100	100	100	100
	40	5	100	100	100	100
	45	5	100	100	100	100
	50	5	100	100	100	100
Unprojected Unit Credit, Maximum Deductible	0	—	0	0	0	0
	5	0	16	0	0	0
	10	0	40	0	0	0
	15	0	49	0	0	0
	20	0	58	0	0	0
	25	0	70	0	0	0
	30	0	88	0	0	0
	35	0	100	39	0	0
	40	0	100	100	100	100
	45	0	100	100	100	100
	50	0	100	100	100	100

Unprojected Unit Credit, Minimum ERISA

0	—	0	0	0	0
5	0	0	0	0	0
10	0	5	0	0	0
15	0	16	0	0	0
20	0	30	0	0	0
25	0	47	0	0	0
30	0	71	0	0	0
35	0	90	0	0	0
40	0	100	37	0	0
45	0	100	100	100	23
50	0	100	100	100	100

Unit Credit with No Trend or Discount Rate, Maximum Deductible

0	—	0	0	0	0
5	0	58	0	0	0
10	0	100	16	0	0
15	0	100	80	0	0
20	0	100	100	62	38
25	0	100	100	100	100
30	0	100	100	100	100
35	0	100	100	100	100
40	0	100	100	100	100
45	0	100	100	100	100
50	0	100	100	100	100

Projected Unit Credit with 5% Cap on Trend, Maximum Deductible

0	—	0	0	0	0
5	5	40	0	0	0
10	5	74	0	0	0
15	5	92	0	0	0
20	5	100	3	0	0
25	5	100	52	0	0

TABLE D.8 (continued)

Funding Method	Year	Expected Trend	Current Retirees	Vested Employees	Nonvested Employees Accrued benefits[b]	Total benefits
Projected Unit Credit with 5% Cap on Trend, Maximum Deductible (continued)	30	5%	100%	100%	61%	38%
	35	5	100	100	60	38
	40	5	100	100	60	38
	45	5	100	100	60	38
	50	5	100	100	60	38
Unit Credit with No Trend or Discount Rate, Minimum ERISA	0	—	0	0	0	0
	5	0	28	0	0	0
	10	0	53	0	0	0
	15	0	76	0	0	0
	20	0	100	0	0	0
	25	0	100	100	53	33
	30	0	100	100	100	100
	35	0	100	100	100	100
	40	0	100	100	100	100
	45	0	100	100	100	100
	50	0	100	100	100	100
Projected Unit Credit with 5% Cap on Trend, Minimum ERISA	0	—	0	0	0	0
	5	5	15	0	0	0
	10	5	31	0	0	0
	15	5	48	0	0	0
	20	5	67	0	0	0
	25	5	91	0	0	0

30	5	100	100	83	52
35	5	100	100	60	38
40	5	100	100	60	38
45	5	100	100	60	38
50	5	100	100	60	38

[a]Funding ratios shown reflect the proportion of the present value of future benefits, for the given class of employees, that is covered by the current fund.
[b]Accrued benefits are defined here as the pro-rata share of benefits earned to date, assuming benefits are earned ratably from date of hire to date of earliest eligibility for retirement.

TABLE D.9
Funding Scenarios: Illustrative Funding Ratios[a]
Group F—7% Rate of Decline: High Trend Scenario

Funding Method	Year	Expected Trend	Current Retirees	Vested Employees	Nonvested Employees Accrued benefits[b]	Nonvested Employees Total benefits
Entry Age Normal, Maximum Deductible	0	—	0%	0%	0%	0%
	5	9%	100	45	0	0
	10	7	100	100	100	66
	15	6	100	100	100	100
	20	5	100	100	100	100
	25	5	100	100	100	100
	30	5	100	100	100	100
	35	5	100	100	100	100
	40	5	100	100	100	100
	45	5	100	100	100	100
	50	5	100	100	100	100
Projected Unit Credit, Maximum Deductible	0	—	0	0	0	0
	5	9	100	12	0	0
	10	7	100	100	59	35
	15	6	100	100	100	87
	20	5	100	100	98	59
	25	5	100	100	100	97
	30	5	100	100	100	100
	35	5	100	100	100	100
	40	5	100	100	100	100
	45	5	100	100	100	100
	50	5	100	100	100	100

Entry Age Normal, Minimum

0	—	0	0	0	0
5	9	65	0	0	0
10	7	100	22	0	0
15	6	100	99	0	0
20	5	100	100	14	9
25	5	100	100	100	62

ERISA

30	5	100	100	100	100
35	5	100	100	100	100
40	5	100	100	100	100
45	5	100	100	100	100
50	5	100	100	100	100

Projected Unit Credit, Minimum

0	—	0	0	0	0
5	9	60	0	0	0
10	7	100	4	0	0
15	6	100	75	0	0
20	5	100	84	0	0
25	5	100	100	59	36

ERISA

30	5	100	100	100	98
35	5	100	100	100	75
40	5	100	100	100	100
45	5	100	100	100	100
50	5	100	100	100	100

(continued)

TABLE D.9 (continued)

Funding Method	Year	Expected Trend	Current Retirees	Vested Employees	Nonvested Employees Accrued benefits[b]	Nonvested Employees Total benefits
Aggregate	0	—	0%	0%	0%	0%
	5	9%	100	20	0	0
	10	7	100	100	44	26
	15	6	100	100	100	91
	20	5	100	100	100	65
	25	5	100	100	100	100
	30	5	100	100	100	100
	35	5	100	100	100	100
	40	5	100	100	100	100
	45	5	100	100	100	100
	50	5	100	100	100	100
Unprojected Unit Credit, Maximum Deductible	0	—	0	0	0	0
	5	0	16	0	0	0
	10	0	39	0	0	0
	15	0	47	0	0	0
	20	0	51	0	0	0
	25	0	62	0	0	0
	30	0	75	0	0	0
	35	0	90	0	0	0
	40	0	100	100	76	48
	45	0	100	100	100	100
	50	0	100	100	100	100

	Unprojected Unit Credit, Minimum ERISA			
0	0	—	0	0
5	5	0	0	0
10	10	0	5	0
15	15	0	16	0
20	20	0	27	0
25	25	0	40	0
30	30	0	58	0
35	35	0	73	0
40	40	0	100	0
45	45	0	100	9
50	50	0	100	98
			100	100

[a] Funding ratios shown reflect the proportion of the present value of future benefits, for the given class of employees, that is covered by the current fund.
[b] Accrued benefits are defined here as the pro-rata share of benefits earned to date, assuming benefits are earned ratably from date of hire to date of earliest eligibility for retirement.

TABLE D.10
Funding Scenarios: Illustrative Funding Ratios[a]
Group H: Low Trend Scenario

Funding Method	Year	Expected Trend	Current Retirees	Vested Employees	Nonvested Employees Accrued benefits[b]	Nonvested Employees Total benefits
Entry Age Normal, Maximum Deductible	0	—	0%	0%	0%	0%
	5	9%	100	100	83	32
	10	7	100	100	100	52
	15	6	100	100	94	46
	20	5	100	100	79	41
	25	5	100	100	71	37
	30	5	100	100	67	34
	35	5	100	100	67	33
	40	5	100	100	68	33
	45	5	100	100	69	34
	50	5	100	100	69	35
Projected Unit Credit, Maximum Deductible	0	—	0	0	0	0
	5	9	100	100	66	25
	10	7	100	100	97	43
	15	6	100	100	77	38
	20	5	100	100	65	34
	25	5	100	100	66	34
	30	5	100	100	63	32
	35	5	100	100	63	31
	40	5	100	100	64	31
	45	5	100	100	64	32
	50	5	100	100	64	32

Entry Age Normal, Minimum

ERISA						
0	0	—	0	0	0	0
5	5	9	100	100	68	26
10	10	7	100	100	100	52
15	15	6	100	100	94	46
20	20	5	100	100	79	41
25	25	5	100	100	70	37
30	30	5	100	100	66	33
35	35	5	100	100	66	33
40	40	5	100	100	67	33
45	45	5	100	100	68	34
50	50	5	100	100	69	34

Projected Unit Credit, Minimum

ERISA						
0	0	—	0	0	0	0
5	5	9	100	100	56	21
10	10	7	100	100	97	43
15	15	6	100	100	77	38
20	20	5	100	100	65	34
25	25	5	100	100	66	34
30	30	5	100	100	63	32
35	35	5	100	100	63	31
40	40	5	100	100	64	31
45	45	5	100	100	64	32
50	50	5	100	100	64	32

(continued)

TABLE D.10 (continued)

Funding Method	Year	Expected Trend	Current Retirees	Vested Employees	Nonvested Employees Accrued benefits[b]	Total benefits
Aggregate	0	—	0%	0%	0%	0%
	5	9%	100	100	65	25
	10	7	100	100	100	51
	15	6	100	100	93	45
	20	5	100	100	77	40
	25	5	100	100	65	34
	30	5	100	100	55	28
	35	5	100	100	50	25
	40	5	100	100	49	24
	45	5	100	100	48	24
	50	5	100	100	46	23
Unprojected Unit Credit, Maximum Deductible	0	—	0	0	0	0
	5	0	100	29	0	0
	10	0	100	21	0	0
	15	0	100	15	0	0
	20	0	100	23	0	0
	25	0	100	20	0	0
	30	0	100	17	0	0
	35	0	100	15	0	0
	40	0	100	11	0	0
	45	0	100	16	0	0
	50	0	100	21	0	0

	Unprojected Unit Credit, Minimum ERISA				
0	0	—	0	0	0
5	0	0	100	4	0
10	0	0	100	2	0
15	0	0	100	1	0
20	0	0	100	2	0
25	0	0	100	1	0
30	0	0	100	1	0
35	0	0	100	1	0
40	0	0	97	0	0
45	0	0	100	0	0
50	0	0	100	1	0

[a] Funding ratios shown reflect the proportion of the present value of future benefits, for the given class of employees, that is covered by the current fund.
[b] Accrued benefits are defined here as the pro-rata share of benefits earned to date, assuming benefits are earned ratably from date of hire to date of earliest eligibility for retirement.

TABLE D.11
Funding Scenarios: Illustrative Funding Ratios[a]
Group H: Medium Trend Scenario

Funding Method	Year	Expected Trend	Current Retirees	Vested Employees	Nonvested Employees Accrued benefits[b]	Nonvested Employees Total benefits
Entry Age Normal, Maximum Deductible	0	—	0%	0%	0%	0%
	5	9%	100	100	66	24
	10	7	100	100	79	33
	15	6	100	100	77	35
	20	5	100	100	76	37
	25	5	100	100	74	37
	30	5	100	100	69	35
	35	5	100	100	67	33
	40	5	100	100	68	33
	45	5	100	100	69	34
	50	5	100	100	69	34
Projected Unit Credit, Maximum Deductible	0	—	0	0	0	0
	5	9	100	100	51	19
	10	7	100	100	64	27
	15	6	100	100	65	30
	20	5	100	100	66	32
	25	5	100	100	66	33
	30	5	100	100	63	32
	35	5	100	100	63	31
	40	5	100	100	64	31
	45	5	100	100	64	32
	50	5	100	100	64	32

Entry Age Normal, Minimum
ERISA

0	—	0	0	0	0
5	9	100	100	52	19
10	7	100	100	78	33
15	6	100	100	77	35
20	5	100	100	76	37
25	5	100	100	74	37
30	5	100	100	69	35
35	5	100	100	67	33
40	5	100	100	67	33
45	5	100	100	68	34
50	5	100	100	68	34

Projected Unit Credit, Minimum
ERISA

0	—	0	0	0	0
5	9	100	100	42	15
10	7	100	100	63	26
15	6	100	100	65	30
20	5	100	100	66	32
25	5	100	100	66	33
30	5	100	100	63	32
35	5	100	100	63	31
40	5	100	100	64	31
45	5	100	100	64	32
50	5	100	100	64	32

(continued)

TABLE D.11 (continued)

Funding Method	Year	Expected Trend	Current Retirees	Vested Employees	Nonvested Employees Accrued benefits[b]	Nonvested Employees Total benefits
Aggregate	0	—	0%	0%	0%	0%
	5	9%	100	100	50	18
	10	7	100	100	74	31
	15	6	100	100	77	35
	20	5	100	100	76	37
	25	5	100	100	74	37
	30	5	100	100	69	35
	35	5	100	100	60	30
	40	5	100	100	55	27
	45	5	100	100	52	26
	50	5	100	100	49	25
Unprojected Unit Credit, Maximum Deductible	0	—	0	0	0	0
	5	0	100	18	0	0
	10	0	100	5	0	0
	15	0	92	0	0	0
	20	0	95	0	0	0
	25	0	100	2	0	0
	30	0	100	16	0	0
	35	0	100	16	0	0
	40	0	100	12	0	0
	45	0	100	17	0	0
	50	0	100	22	0	0

Unprojected Unit Credit, Minimum ERISA	0	—	0	0	0
	5	0	100	0	0
	10	0	93	2	0
	15	0	81	0	0
	20	0	83	0	0
	25	0	90	0	0
	30	0	100	0	0
	35	0	100	0	0
	40	0	98	0	0
	45	0	100	0	0
	50	0	100	2	0
Unit Credit with No Trend or Discount Rate, Maximum Deductible	0	—	0	0	0
	5	0	100	100	5
	10	0	100	100	6
	15	0	100	100	15
	20	0	100	100	32
	25	0	100	100	53
	30	0	100	100	80
	35	0	100	100	79
	40	0	100	100	78
	45	0	100	100	78
	50	0	100	100	79
Projected Unit Credit with 5% Cap on Trend, Maximum Deductible	0	—	0	0	0
	5	5	100	100	1
	10	5	100	71	0
	15	5	100	85	0
	20	5	100	100	6
	25	5	100	100	29

(continued)

TABLE D.11 (continued)

					Nonvested Employees	
Funding Method	Year	Expected Trend	Current Retirees	Vested Employees	Accrued benefits[b]	Total benefits
Projected Unit Credit with 5% Cap on Trend, Maximum Deductible (continued)	30	5%	100%	100%	62%	31%
	35	5	100	100	63	31
	40	5	100	100	64	31
	45	5	100	100	64	32
	50	5	100	100	64	32
Unit Credit with No Trend or Discount Rate, Minimum	0	—	0	0	0	0
ERISA	5	0	100	100	8	3
	10	0	100	100	6	3
	15	0	100	100	26	12
	20	0	100	100	59	29
	25	0	100	100	100	53
	30	0	100	100	100	80
	35	0	100	100	100	79
	40	0	100	100	100	78
	45	0	100	100	100	78
	50	0	100	100	100	79
Projected Unit Credit with 5% Cap on Trend, Minimum	0	—	0	0	0	0
ERISA	5	5	100	83	0	0
	10	5	100	58	0	0
	15	5	100	72	0	0
	20	5	100	99	0	0
	25	5	100	100	23	12

30	5	100	100	57	29
35	5	100	100	63	31
40	5	100	100	64	31
45	5	100	100	64	32
50	5	100	100	64	32

[a] Funding ratios shown reflect the proportion of the present value of future benefits, for the given class of employees, that is covered by the current fund.
[b] Accrued benefits are defined here as the pro-rata share of benefits earned to date, assuming benefits are earned ratably from date of hire to date of earliest eligibility for retirement.

TABLE D.12
Funding Scenarios: Illustrative Funding Ratios[a]
Group H: High Trend Scenario

Funding Method	Year	Expected Trend	Current Retirees	Vested Employees	Nonvested Employees Accrued benefits[b]	Nonvested Employees Total benefits
Entry Age Normal, Maximum Deductible	0	—	0%	0%	0%	0%
	5	9%	100	100	66	24
	10	7	100	100	85	36
	15	6	100	100	100	54
	20	5	100	100	77	36
	25	5	100	100	84	41
	30	5	100	100	100	51
	35	5	100	100	70	34
	40	5	100	100	70	34
	45	5	100	100	69	34
	50	5	100	100	69	34
Projected Unit Credit, Maximum Deductible	0	—	0	0	0	0
	5	9	100	100	51	19
	10	7	100	100	65	27
	15	6	100	100	100	46
	20	5	100	100	67	31
	25	5	100	100	73	36
	30	5	100	100	94	46
	35	5	100	100	64	30
	40	5	100	100	64	31
	45	5	100	100	64	32
	50	5	100	100	64	32

Entry Age Normal, Minimum

ERISA	0	—	0	0	0	0
	5	9	100	100	52	19
	10	7	100	100	79	33
	15	6	100	100	100	54
	20	5	100	100	77	36
	25	5	100	100	84	41
	30	5	100	100	100	51
	35	5	100	100	70	34
	40	5	100	100	70	34
	45	5	100	100	69	34
	50	5	100	100	68	34

Projected Unit Credit, Minimum

ERISA	0	—	0	0	0	0
	5	9	100	100	42	15
	10	7	100	100	63	27
	15	6	100	100	100	46
	20	5	100	100	67	31
	25	5	100	100	73	36
	30	5	100	100	94	46
	35	5	100	100	64	30
	40	5	100	100	64	31
	45	5	100	100	64	32
	50	5	100	100	64	32

(continued)

TABLE D.12 (continued)

Funding Method	Year	Expected Trend	Current Retirees	Vested Employees	Nonvested Employees Accrued benefits[b]	Total benefits
	0	—	0%	0%	0%	0%
Aggregate						
	5	9%	100	100	50	18
	10	7	100	100	79	33
	15	6	100	100	100	54
	20	5	100	100	77	36
	25	5	100	100	83	41
	30	5	100	100	100	50
	35	5	100	100	68	33
	40	5	100	100	70	34
	45	5	100	100	61	30
	50	5	100	100	56	28

[a] Funding ratios shown reflect the proportion of the present value of future benefits, for the given class of employees, that is covered by the current fund.
[b] Accrued benefits are defined here as the pro-rata share of benefits earned to date, assuming benefits are earned ratably from date of hire to date of earliest eligibility for retirement.